Infinite Poetry
By
Albert Carrasco
aka
Infinite the Poet

Infinite Poetry
Copyright © 2012 by Albert "Infinite The Poet" Carrasco
alcarrasco2@yahoo.com

Cover design by Chyna Blue for Edifyin' Graphix

Published by Hip Hope Publishing
hiphopepublishing@gmail.com

ISBN- 978-0-9834739-2-3

Without limiting the rights under the copyright reserved above, no part of this publication may be reproduced, stored in or introduced into retrieval system, or transmitted, in any form, or by any means, without the prior written permission of the copyright owner and publisher of this book.

This book is dedicated to my wife, Sharon B. Carrasco and my mother, Zoraida "Sherry" Carrasco

"Your son did it."

~~~

I would like to thank my family, friends and fans for believing in me, for listening to me and for reading my visions. If it wasn't for all of you, there would be no Infinite The Poet! Thank you very much. I promise to continue to try to change lives through words.

Table Of Contents

Who Is Al Carrasco?	Build And Destroy
Me	My Infinite Symbol
1984	Driving Out Of Poverty
Trend	The Ghetto Poetical Alto
Military	A Slave
Hustlers Of Culture	Dangerous Blocks
I Been Shot	The Result Of A Gun Shot
David's Bridal	Mr. Street
Things Have Changed	Ms. Streets
Crooked Letter	A Serenade
Stages In Ten	A Letter To My Dead Friends
Tradition	Life In The Hood
Under The Same Sky	Al Carrasco, Revolutionary
In The A.M.	White Girl
Being Bullied	Dad, Can I Ask You A Question?
Forgiveness	These Two People
Child Abuse	Projects
A Survivor	A Kid's View
Just Not My Eyes	The Crying River
A Mother's Fear	Good Times
Trapped	A 12 Year Old
Time	Kumbaya, My Lord
The Darkness	The System
Da Bronx	Action And Reaction
Perdon, Madre Mia	That Phone Call
Build And Destroy	Science
My Infinite Symbol	My Imagination
Driving Out Of Poverty	A Victim To Know The Ledge
The Ghetto Poetical Alto	After Nine Months

Click Clack

I Want To Be Just Like Him

In Your Head

John Doe

Stuck In The Middle

The Mirror

The Pain In My Pen

The Window

Thoughts

Roaming

My Arrival

Guns

It's So Hard

Attempt To Assassinate My Character

Flower For The Dead

Knock, Knocked

Mask

Two Different Trips, Although Sounding Like Similar Stories

Veterans

Who Is Albert Carrasco?

Albert Carrasco is not only a rapper and spoken word artist, but also a motivational speaker of sorts, using his words to uplift young people faced with the same difficult life choices as he was. Growing up in the Bronx, New York, Carrasco lost his father at age 12 and within four years he was arrested, shot twice and dealing drugs. He saw so many of his friends die off and he couldn't stand the idea of his newborn son growing up into that life, so 11 years ago, Carrasco turned his life around.

He began to write poetry as a release, tapping into the harsh lyrical honesty that continues to permeate his music. "I write about religion, poverty, basically anything young people are going through," said Carrasco, who proved to be an anomaly on the spoken word circuit with his unique subject matter. "This is what I saw in my life. I'm speaking from reality, not from my imagination." At the behest of a friend, Carrasco made his spoken word debut at the Nuyorican Poetry Cafe and continues to appear at open mics throughout New York City to rapturous response from the crowds.

Carrasco's first album, "On the Wrong Path to the Riches", debut in 2010, fusing spoken word and rap to make a new genre all his own. On it, the now-married father of three, raps on 11 acapella and R&B-based tracks produced by R. Twice and Max Perez. Carrasco also serves as the guest vocalist on "Wake Up", the first single from Perez, new as-yet-untitled album, due out in 2012.

Me

writing is a passion deep inside of me
caged up so anxious to be released
words not spoken can't feed a thirsty mind waiting to eat
so I've decided to speak to the ones that wanna be fed
instead of holding these thoughts inside my head

you see my vision of happiness was chasing money
being a drug seller or a gun runner
anything to keep my pockets full I did for the capital
at sixteen, I was shot twice
took two for the team
but in the emergency room I lay there like,
damn all this for that cream
I was too blind to see what the pursuit of currency
was doing to me
at this time, I should of realized I was on the wrong
path to the riches
in the ER undergoing surgery and getting stitches
I walk around with a bullet to this day
but to me, for that cash, it's a small price to pay
even out the hospital doors I'm on the phone trying
to make my money soar
blinded to what this game had in store

cars, jewelry, stick up kids trying to do me,
groupies in line trying to screw me,
living life like a movie
no script, no actors
real men of my stature didn't surrender
the thought of possessing that legal tender
celebrity stats, fully auto gats cause me to wear
kevlar on my back
32 shot clips, stash box in whips, blinding light in
rear to disappear when danger was near
it was a catastrophic curriculum
where I'm from in the slums to sell drugs
and bust guns cause of the fear of being bums

isolated from the real world
we continued the life style that we knew
banging and hanging in our housing vestibule
living life by our rules
advice by others not needed and when it was given
it wasn't heeded
now I still got cash but time has taken precious
things from me
friends I rolled with and shared my bliss
most are dead and so dearly missed
it is what it is, I can't change what was written
this game is full of snakes and even the strongest get bitten
bad decisions in search of fame in this game will leave u lifeless
well, I was smart and decisive in a game that's as cold
as is fun in this life didn't last for some
was like speeding in a car till it ran out of gas to them
my tank was always full and I kept a chauffeur
living the life of la costra nostra

inner city kids in an inner city struggle with no direction
just the ghettos reflection of kids needing attention
time has passed by so fast
just like most of the guys I lost in this oppression
I continue to live life with the few that are still alive
for different goals we strive
no more fast life
we're taking slow strides
no more funerals to make moms and wives cry
all I wanted was not to be poor
not to have my friends sent early knocking on
heaven's door
the choices that are made, as a kid, sometimes devastate
us as adults
so I want the youth to see that the game is really fantasy
so those that looked up to me in the streets, I want them to
continue to look up to me
but for something positive not cause the life I lived
so I'll share my scars
my losses and my bad choices

to enlighten a few on what this game will bring
the street history is a story of destruction, corruption,
a pattern of misery
at 40, I'm still feeling the wrath of that passed life I lived in
waiting anxiously for a few to be released from prison
17, 20, 40 year bids for things we did as kids
the game ended for me and a few, but there's still those
to have to see their sentence through
you know how sad it is to see the children of my fallen
soldiers grow up without a father
my father died when I was twelve and so did my
childhood
so their outlook on life to me is very sadly understood

1984

welcome to the year 1984 when the era of crack came
and caused mass hysteria
one of the places it hit hard was our area
this substance was highly addictive
not just to the users, but to the pusher
they got higher, we got richer
they loved the feeling of it taking over their mind
I loved the money, it helped me leave poor life behind

an incomplete cipher, a recipe for disaster, but I
kept brewing
cooking the things these fiends were abusing
I got sucked in, because of the situation I was in
dad dying, moms struggling, little brothers crying,
older brother caught up as well
we are both trying
we are both leos, hearts of lions
the odds; we defied them
the streets, we confided in them

guns blast, blood baths, sirens flash, disturbing
aftermaths
losing so many soldiers through the years
my peers doing federal and state time
being moved state to state, jail to jail, tier to tier
for living life with hope, not fear

from kids kidding to men bidding
we kept dreaming the dream of being rich
dreams are just thoughts while we are sleeping
sometimes they're misleading or did I just wake
up early so I didn't see all my men bleeding

this life was a travesty
life's reality left us to live in fantasy
it's a tragedy to live life with blind strategies
standing on drug corners feeling we are dominant

youths killing youths just to say respect our conglomerate

drug sales, pistols, death, jail
the hope of being rich
99 percent fail

even with the odds, we tried to live in that
1 percentile
failure wasn't optional
after growing up poor feeling pain in your
abdominal
it's no problem to grab packs and walk the
avenue in search of revenue
it was our way out

kids going to war
not in the military, in the streets
kids getting killed and the killer being sent
to solitary
it's a ghetto documentary that's been filmed
and continues to be filmed to this day
just with different people that decided
to play

these streets really persuade the youngsters to
pursue the path
that was laid by their forefathers in the drug trade
we learned how to cut, cook, and manufacture the
substance that destroyed so many lives
caught up in a rapture, living life in a unnatural
disaster
living in this circumstance sometimes was too hard
to muster
we took it all in instead of all of our family suffering

local kids that became friends, that became a local
drug gang died at the same rate as the disease
following hiv
killing for colors of the spectrum, r.o.y g. b.I.v.

rico laws, king pin charges is what we faced
after years behind bars, for a second chance
we say grace

kite sending, commissary, open cases pending,
lawyers, DAs
us vs. the people
repetitive actions made this a sequel
the games made only for the extraordinary
or the ones that are born in, inherently
meaning their moms or pops or siblings were
into the same get rich schemes
get money by any means

buildings built together on a four corner block
filled with misguided adolescents
went to war for the rock under false pretenses
life was like a western, wild cowboys in gun battles
in broad daylight with no sheriffs there to arrest us
after the gun fight

neighboring lobbies became local drug dens
shoot outs to defend drug turf being scouted by
other men
we all have stab wounds and bullet holes if you
was lucky
the unlucky had funerals
those sights disgust me
it's disgusting how I saw my friends with
glued, shut jaws
and most of their insides removed
in that life this is fluent
for 3 days you see a body preserved
with embalming fluid

we lived by the phrase "we don't die,
we multiply!"
it just didn't add up
a lot of people were dying, parents crying

I had to leave the game I was fed up
a huge time of my life was spent sacrificing
other lives to live in so called paradise

my paradise isn't from what I earned in the game
money or fame
it's the love for and from my family
I wish I could of realized that before the crack
epidemic came that was 84
now it's 2010
I'm glad that era came to an end
and since then, I promised not to sacrifice no
more of my men

Trend

I grew up the youngest out of a close knit band of brothers
out to discover what the streets had to offer
what we found was a way to stop us from being hungry
which led to the thirst of money
gang banging and trapping
whichever way we tried to make it happen

kids living lavish off of drug blocks we established
lived off the assumption we will continue this status
rocks in low fire for Cubans with Lazarus pieces
chrome rims with low pro tires to handle these
sport car screeches
leather gloves for the stick ups and the stick shift
from slipping
we all had water on the neck dripping
rolexes silently ticking, puffing on the piff or sour
all color ice on the wrist we called it piragua

mug shots, fingerprints, foot ball numbers,
for being infiltrated by under covers
hand to hand transactions being recorded
and captioned
secret indictments got half the block missing
in action
leaving gaps for people to fall into the trap
thinking since they're gone that their next up to bat
once you see the money you can't leave it alone
some will strip flesh from bone to earn money
for a home
some will sell that deadly mix
brewed by the ghetto chemist
searched by fiends looking for that 10 minute fix
catching cases praying those 220 charges don't stick

some think they reign supreme until they are arraigned
in supreme court with their cohorts for this street life sport

life behind bars is nothing we sought
but was a probability we hoped to never face
capitol murder killing for money the ultimate case

central booking is like a ghetto museum
the ghetto is like one big mausoleum
most people that live there die there
before finding a way out if we do
most get caught up in the turbulence
of the people
that was living fast in our past
feeling there's nothing else we followed
the same path

guys from across the street from each other compete
for blocks that we would never own
trying to rise in the ranks of the street hierarchy
we lived in anarchy trying to be the ones with
the most clientele
the ones whose names rang bells
we became the ones that filled jails
the ones that interior designed cells for sales
because we couldn't post bail
our dream of being rich failed

stuck between a rock and a hard place after
incarceration and being tagged as felons
our search for legal dividends came to dead ends
because of our past situations of illegal narcotics
selling
no one wanted us in their dwelling
so we continue our journey that most likely
ends in gurneys, blood transfusions,
intravenous feeding
electrical chest presses if the heart stops beating
porta potties strapped to people's bodies so they can
urinate from a hole in their abdomen
this tragically keeps on happening chasing the high
of street life passion

and after the guns start blasting
nickel and diming, entrepreneurs enterprising
advertising their goods
up to no good destroyed our hoods
ability to rise over our label "projects"
insufficient guidance led to violence
insufficient knowledge led to blindness
misconstrued visions, a prelude to bad decisions
a domino effect that left us in prisons
made by most in the projects, we were imprisoned

destined to fail, we strive for success
not wanting to live average
we ran with the same ideas that dead men left
thinking we will do it better
we were much more clever,
but got the same outcome
jail, coroners, another mom losing a son

my friends' bodies filled cemeteries
like confetti after a celebration
we wasn't celebrating
we was looking for emancipation from
the poor life classification

hustled for personification, which led to
courtroom sessions
and more funeral processions
most of our plans ended with flower arrangements
for lost brothers, bereavement

I've been internally crying even though on my
exterior you see me smiling
just trying to hide the terror inside me and
stay law abiding
my actions from the past haunt me now
it's hell's aftermath
I feel solo in this world that's so cold
like my homies felt with no soul

so cold rigor mortis for being hard body
almost lost everybody
for living life like one big party

Military

when I was young, I wanted to go to military school but
daddy died and alone mom couldn't pay tuition
I knew I was special didn't want to follow tradition
go to public school, dropout, and not have a pot to piss in
so since I couldn't go to military school, to the streets I enlisted
although not in military school but public school
I kept the fascination of guns in the ninth grade
I got arrested for a shotty so there I go to Spofford
in a juvy is where they threw me
coming out of the juvy without telling on the people
that gave me the gun made it easier to get
another one
I knew the code of the street was to remain silent
or become a morgue's next client
so I didn't speak
didn't wanna be covered in a white sheet with
a toe tag on my feet forever asleep
my name is ringing bells
so many stories people tell but none are
accurate
nobody can tell my story of glory but me
even though I don't like to brag and boast
I had more than most but I kept low key

I ran around with the kids that were just like me
very trust worthy and the same goals
money, power and hoes
triple beam dreams, jewelry, cars and clothes
we all clicked labeled our clique the bellacos

from nickel and diming we began enterprising
and organizing in the drug and gun game
we was terrorizing because not being poor anymore
was so satisfying
the bond, us kids had, for another was so strong
if u saw one of us, there was definitely two or three
of us close by tagging along

when I was sixteen I was so lucky to be amongst
a few members of my team
a friend of mines had some problems
so of course we go with him to solve them
but it just didn't work that way
now we are used to gun play
but that day the gun was being pointed my
way and the gun sprayed
got hit twice, once in the arm and once to the knee
if it wasn't for my man, another day wouldn't
be promised to see
he dives on me and takes one in his neck
almost lost his life and it was me he was trying
to protect, as I lay bleeding profusely
on a cold concrete floor out my wounds the blood
continues to pour
I'm in shock, I gather enough strength to pick up
myself and my boy
we jump in the car and head to Montefiore

the ride to the hospital was 5 minutes away but
it felt like forever
while me and my man lay bleeding on the car's
leather
my friend's gunshot wound was a in and out
not me I wasn't that lucky
I got shot once in the knee
but the one that did harm was the one shot
to my arm
because it traveled into my chest and stopped by
my lung
mom didn't know how close she was to losing
a son

after getting shot I became so violent
wasn't gonna get shot first ever again
instead I'll let my gun burst first trying to
defend my men
coming out of the hospital I couldn't even stand

up straight
it took about six months to recuperate
I was missing a chunk of meat from my right
knee and my arm was shattered
I couldn't even lift a bar of soap
at that time life was so hard to cope
me and Edgar was the first to get shot on
our team
fortunately we survived
unfortunately, it wasn't the same for peers
I would lose them all in the upcoming
years

Ralphy shot 5 times
Orlando shot 2 times
Bunca shot 2 times
Edgar stabbed once
Caddy Dave shot 5 times
Koko shot 1 time
Eddie shot 1 time
Kris Kringle shot 1 time
Blue shot one time
6 months ago, my man locked up 17 years
came home and died in his sleep
Adbul Gaffer Abdul

Rest in peace

Hustlers Of Culture

I'm from a culture of hustlers that hustled culture
we tried to reach the top so we circled the grounds
like eagles and vultures
we preyed, we was prey
this is a phyla and sub phyla way,
                                      bosses
                     Managers
                                            Steerers

                  Pitchers
                             Street dreamers

we wanted to be leaders
so did killers, so blood leaks by the liter
blood leaked so much on these project streets
you can't notice because it's covered with crack vials,
dope glassines, guts from dutchies, dog waste, as well as, human feces,
all sorts of litter camouflaged the scene of a murder

nickel and diming turned into monopolizing and
organizing
which turned into jail and death
being at the wrong place and the wrong time is
the start of a whole lot of crying
then, a domino effect
the killer gets killed, the kin of the killer seeks revenge
another life ends, then another, then another
sisters, as well as brothers, fathers, as well as mothers, everyone
wants a message sent
from youthful offenders to elderly defendants
we all defended our dependents without remorse
or resentment
no cheek for a cheek, it was eye for an eye
it was slugs in clips in guns
it's called the slums
some make bail and chill

some do time in population come home on
parole
then it's back to population control
dark angels walking in and out of the devil's
threshold
blind man's ego

I lived to see all this happening
it's like living in Armageddon witnessing the
apocalypse in housing projects
I see a collage of images embedded in my mind
like ghetto hieroglyphics
I see mouths wide open, I know they're screaming
along with these images I imagine what I'm hearing
it's eerie, as my mental manifests thoughts with sound,
that's why I say they're screaming
I could be in church and these thoughts continue streaming
it's like my mind has a wifi connection to horror TV, movies
I'm an enigma, a walking cinema
I'm multi-complexed
I have a vision of perplexed inclinations
I write dispositions with predilection from
the thoughts I preprocessed as a preteen
these are reality vaccines from the ghetto PHD
instead of suma cum laude
I thank god I graduated from the streets of
hard knocks sooner than later

I need no scalpel to dissect, nor needle to stitch wounds
my pen cuts deep while my ink heals the weak
I was born at 7 months, my birthday is on the 7th
month
I guess out mamma's womb birth the 7th son
I'm here to save my younger counterparts
warrior get out of poverty
brave hearts, I know how it starts
I know how it stops
a dream then a plot brewing that street potion
leads to teenage abortion not from pregnancy

I'm using abortion as a metaphor
I'm talking about the recoil of metal-fours and fives
and nines
the reason why young kids die and the reason adults
try hard to live
the world needs my words
please heed my words, or it's obituary after
your dead - words

I Been Shot

adrenaline pumping…in shock…I'm aware
I'm aware but all I can do is stare
I see a light's glare as I try to reach out and grab
my motor skills are short circuited
I can feel my body being pricked but there's no pain
am I dead or am I alive on death's doorstep?
if I'm alive, I'm barely living
can't hear or feel myself breathing
can't feel the blood leaking
the red color on white sheets proved I
was bleeding
blood gushing out of a hole in my arm
down my elbow
it was dripping

what makes us tick is on the floor clotting
it's getting thick
darkness then light, light then darkness
I continue to go in and out of consciousness
I'm in the ultimate battle for life
my own survival plight
I see a woman's face distorted but I see her

blond hair blue eyes
tears dripping down her cheek
mouth moving but can't hear her speak

she's squeezing my hand but I can't feel
the squeeze
she drops to her knees
in that instance I came through as I can feel pain
I see I'm on a hospital bed holding a crucifix chain
the light was operating table lights
the blond haired, blue eyed lady on her knees
was my mom fainting
after begging the lord not to take me
I was shot!!

David's Bridal

the sounds of gun shots
then yells and sirens
caution tape, coroners
somebody died is a fact none the less
white sheets over a body, forever asleep
black books are out while they eyed the crowd
did you see what happened?
everybody's mute
no one knows why there's a body with multiple holes
like a flute
an elderly woman arrives on the scene
she wants to confirm what she's overheard
homicide removes the sheets for her to peek
she screams: how and why!
It was her worst nightmare to see her
boy die
they explain it was a drug transaction
gone array
he got shot 3 times--2 to the torso and one
between the eyes
tears jerk, cops have no witnesses to the perps
this guy that lays on the floor
his moms has to tell her grand children daddy
is not coming around no more
one is a couple of months and the other is four
dad was only twenty five but he stopped aging
an hour after he walked out the door
the time is 4, moms has no clue what's in store
she left about 2
she had an appointment at this special store
she tries outfit after outfit to get that perfect look
and fit
she finds it
they press it and bag it
it really didn't need any alterations
back to home she races
on the way upstairs she sees some

neighbors
they usually say hi
today, it's grim faces
she puts her key in the tumbler
but the police open the door for her
she sees her kids crying
mother on the floor laying
they try to console her
then they told "her"
your husband has just been
murdered
she's dumbfounded
and she immediately weeps
as she drops to her knees
the package she was carrying that says
"David's Bridal" falls by her feet
she's screaming, "no please god we were
getting married next week"
he said he was gonna do a deal
I begged him before I left not to go
he insisted it was money for our limo

Things Have Changed

wow, how things have changed
instead of being home writing this
I would of been hustling in 2125 lobby
with my 4 fifth opening the door for everybody
looking out for everybody
so nobody called po po on me
telling them I'm selling heron and 5 dollar felonies
they saw me grow, "Al, go upstairs and eat"
nah, it's ok I know how to deal with hunger
and my clientele crossing the street
I ate breakfast lunch and dinner looking
out the hallway window
watching for fiends and foot patrol
skeeeyuuu, I'm up here…they come up…
I tell them copp and go
such a snafu
I lost so much, lost so many
not looking for credibility but for stability
we hustled death and lost life
our days were cut short due to the fast life
nights and fatal gun fights
we had no skills unless you was talking
about cooking coke to crack
or how to graduate from grams to a kilo
before getting "left back"
or charged with the rico by 12 peered people
such a snafu
now I hustle scrolls of an urban lost soul
I now manifest what manifested in housing projects
to intercept illegal profit
I teach all about the games Armageddon before
it actually happens
I can explain the pain of being shot without
the gun actually clapping
I can save the youth from becoming 'missing in action'
Infinite the Poet is my name, remember it
I'm gonna snafu the game

Crooked letter

why do I have to stand here with these cracks
in my hand from dusk till dawn?
that's me asking myself that question
why do I always get jumped out on by un-uniformed
risking my freedom?
why do I have to wake up at 8 to be in criminal or
supreme court by 9:30 to look at calendars
to see what arraignment room hell begins for either
trial by judge or by jury
when it's a felony those are two options
bail and bond became my life's ransom
lawyers and DAs are the peoples' politicians
fighting for money or trying to incriminate us
off of hear-say
either we go free or go in the pen as youths
and come out men to repeat the days of yesterday
why am I so good at being bad?
why am I following the footprints of my dad when I
know they'll lead me to his plaque surrounded by
dirt and grass?
why was everyone around me happy I was a dealer
except for my mother?
was it because they was ok with me sacrificing my life
so they didn't have to suffer?
why why why why why?????
is a question by the deaf, dumb, and blind
so I no longer ask why… why?
because my three eyes are opened wide

Stages In Ten

birth - it was 1971
my dad was a soldier fresh out of Vietnam
my mother was a military nurse
a few years after their tour, from the sperm in
dad's scrotum to mom's fallopian
seven months later I was born
I was sucking on mom's titi being born a premi
moms constantly had to feed and care for me
she kept me healthy
she had good practice, she had one before me
my brother Sidney, he was also born premature so
moms already knew what was in store
Moms and dad migrated from Puerto Rico
after I was born we moved to Ohio then
back to New York--Gun Hill
then finally resting in the projects in Castle Hill
that's where things started going downhill
the VA paid, then the VA was late, then the VA
decided to stop dad's pay
moms is now struggling to keep shelter and
food every day
life was becoming harsh and unfair so my honorably
discharged parents now need welfare and health care...

I was ten –
Albert, if you don't clean your room I'm going
to kick your ass
when you finish, brush your teeth, come eat then after
go take out the trash, come back in, then take a bath
ok, mommy
I did everything she said, no hesitation
dad would be silent
I knew he was listening and paying attention
no way in the world would I disrespect them
like I said, my dad was in the military so he raised me
and my brother as service men
moms had my little brother in her belly

when he's born, I'm sure dad will be the same to him
we were so obedient
we never spoke unless spoken to
I was told never to volunteer information
so if you asked me something all you got was
the answer to that one question
nothing more, nothing less
dad was also righteous
Alfred3x
he taught me mathematics to become a
son of Malcolm X
he brought me to Harlem rallies
I remember being placed on the shoulders of
Muhammad Ali
I was raised with discipline. ..

I'm twenty - dad died when I was 12 years old
ten years ago my little brother was born
he doesn't even really remember our dad
my older brother now had be our father
his attitude became darker
he slept by my side every night for years
now I have no clue to where he sleeps
we both were out somewhere claiming ghetto
streets
pop…pop..pop..pop get the fuck off our block
next rounds won't hit the moon, through epidermis,
muscle, then bone is where they'll mushroom
I've been corrupted from poverty and violence,
drugs and guns, hood pestilence
I worshipped the dollar bill
when it was God that should of been trusting
I saw my hero die a slow death, I saw the hurt in his face
it hurt me when he left so I shared my hurt
every place
please don't stop me lil bro and mom from
eating
I'll stop you from breathing, as I comb the Bronx
with my heathens

from ten to twenty, I been incarcerated and shot
multiple times
lost about ten friends of mine
you can't even believe my state of mind....

I'm thirty- death came back to back
lost like ten more friends and put my mother in jail
put my older brother in jail
put my mother's new husband in jail
bureau of child welfare looking for my little brothers
everything failed
I'm sick and tired of courts and jail, bail and bonds
funerals, burials and murals
I got tired of having dividends I couldn't spend
I got tired of my friends sacrificing their lives for a
better way to live
plus now I got my own son and my girl became
my wife
something had to give so I gave up the street
my wife is working while I'm home changing pampers,
mixing Similac bottles,
admiring little hands and feet, as I watch my baby boy sleep
he was my drug intervention
there was one problem, my cash was disappearing
I was being a good daddy, but I wasn't bringing in
cash to help mommy take care of our new family....

I'm forty- now I'm a father of three
I wake up, drop kids to school, get in my truck
and drive to Long Island, to the city, and the Bronx
I'm a survivor
we pay a babysitter for my little girl and school for my
two boys
I'm also a poet, a spoken word artist
I paint pictures of the school of hard knocks
as if I was a professor in college
at the same time I'm giving my peers mental
triage
from the scars that come along with trying

to be drug czars
I'm blessed to be reciting on many different stages in
different areas to get my point across
I have a lyrical way of saving my brothers from being
crucified, like my other brother nailed on a cross

Tradition

I was always the underdog
daddy died when I was young so I had to
act like a man around men
but I was a boy
my dad's legacy lived through me
he had lots of respect and I wanted it to
be handed down to me
he labeled me his "ace"
I sucked in everything I saw
he saw the determination on my face
and I didn't care what it was he did
I just wanted to be like him
if he was a barber, I would of cut hair,
if he was a pastor I would of preached,
but he was neither of the two, he was a hustler
he sold hash for cash and sold reefer in three dollar
yellow bags
I don't care what you guys say, he's the best dad
I could of ever had
I stood by his side like a pleat in his jeans so I inherited
his hustling genes
his temper is anger, his swagger
the way I went about making green
inherited the same attempted murder crime scenes
they shot him and they shot me
dad is already dead so he's already upstairs watching
his son going through everything he went through
his angelic heart must of been in despair
sorry, it almost took me to get to the same age as you
when you died before I realized
there was no rainbow on the other side, no gems, no end
you just ride that destructive wave till you die
I was a phenom for selling venom
going to war in the ghetto like you was in
Vietnam
selling suicide bombs of fire like napalm for diamonds
and gold on my arm

a nice rope chain on
then I did what you said never to do
I moved up to her-on
another deadly powdery substance abused
it was supplied in the Bx in abundance destroying our circumference
leading to death, judge and lawyer and DA conferences stamp confrontations
no one wanted others to create an imitation or to lower our distribution and shorten our paper
so I ran wild with nothing else on my mind
but drug capers
it wasn't long before understanding what this drug was doing to families, so I opted out
no more main veining from the stamp I was claiming
no more nose candy to destroy nose cavities
dudes I loved started to use what I was selling for the things I loved
imagine fighting to bring close friends to rehab because they're now smoking crack and giving that vein a tap with a rubber band strap
injecting h20 on a spoon with the contents of a little glassine baggy into a needle
then in their blood the evil is consumed
it weakens the system
and when they don't have it their back hurts
badly
some of my men heated while rotating that
stem
made fiends out of la creme de la creme
many sleepless nights searching for them
many mornings burying, then mourning them
although most of my friends died by the bullet
they all overdosed
no matter how you put it, it all was the effect
of drugs
I guess this was the one thing daddy didn't teach
like I said up top, he died, I survived
so I'm back to preach to that same demographic

the same drug crowd
I just have questions that I know can't be answered
am I still your ace? do I make you proud?

Under The Same Sky

I wake up and thank God I woke up
kiss the forehead of my immediate family
my kids, plus wifey
I stretch, open the blinds, squint my eyes as the sun
is shining brightly
either I'm going to work or writing, doing household chores
or just being lazy behind closed doors
I have options
I can eat breakfast or sleep or wake up to brunch
I can get in my car and travel to and fro as I please
I can follow any idea or hunch, things that I can do,
I have a bunch

I wake up and thank God I woke up
I sleep where and when I can in few minute intervals
we are at war because of roadside bombs and
sniper's nests
yesterday in our platoon we lost four to shrapnel
and slugs that traveled some ways
the killers are unseen so we call for predator drones
or air support teams
my ears ache from the sound of destruction
I hear gun battles even when we're at ease
so much bloodshed I saw pour I can duplicate the red sea

I wake up and thank God I woke up
I hear the CO's calling
wakeup, scumbags and maggots
that's the warden coming
I hardly get to see natural light
can't remember the last time I saw the moon rise
at night
I've seen stabbings, stranglings and days upon days
of fighting
today they switched my celly
he was a first timer now they got me moonlighting
with a murdering repeat offender

he's known as X and he's a three time loser
he says he got it from his father who was an abuser
he said he saw it every day in his mom
his father used to abuse her
so when people upset me, I whoop their ass
my moms must of been lucky because these people
I beat to a pulp
excessive head trauma coroner states that's the
reason three people passed

I wake up and thank God I woke up
they say without food and water that in four
days you'll die
OMG, Lord I feel like I'm dying
I'm so hungry and thirsty
when I do eat or drink… it hurts me
my mother and sister went to the well with buckets
to pump water
but it was dry and they come home empty handed
not to our surprise
that's why the starvation death rate is hitting
an all time high
I get emotional
not just me, I'm 5
but momma also has a 2 year old
we're crying but you can't see
no water mixed with sodium drops from our
cheeks
we are dehydrated
day three of no water and nothing to eat
mammas breast milk evaporated so lil sis
can't even suck on her titti
why are we so poor, can someone tell me why?
this is a vision of different lives under the same sky

In the A.M.

the birds chirped, I opened my eyes and reached under
the bed to feel for my cash
then I feel for mama's plate
the night before last I bagged a bomb so when those
birds chirped
it was like my marathon alarm
it was time to run the track, blood cap enclosed crack,
45 extended clips kept the stick up kids fallen back
if not on impulse I attacked, pitty pat
hollows ripping through flack
then on point waiting to see if they dare follow
with a retaliatory attack
I ignored all my mom's wishes
every thirty goes ten mixed in those pyrex dishes
screaming mom mind your business!
she tried to warn me
tried to tell me drugs ruins families
I didn't listen now a slug is part of my anatomy
for my street life analogy
thought I was an anomaly
really I was just a tiny statistic of the majority
caught up in the monotony of trying to illegally
earn a monopoly
guess what?
moms went to jail because of me
her life was hell because of me
the guys that rode with me now rest underneath
studying botany like scientists
I could of been pushing up daisies
when the devil aimed for me, the lord snatched me
out of his cross hairs and saved mom's second
baby
so how do I thank the man upstairs?
I stand in front of crowds, standing up the people
sitting in chairs hairs
watch teary eyed stares while they hear my story
of a young guy trying to get rich for living so long

in poverty and what it cost me
all the souls the street stole from me was costly

Being Bullied

damn there they go again
the same guys
I want to turn around and walk the other direction
I just don't want them to think I'm a wuss
I'm not scared, I just don't like problems
they are problems!
we had a few run ins in the past and it was always
after my math class
while I stroll the second floor's corridor path
it started with pointing of the fingers, to brushing of the
shoulders, to them trying to trip me
one even spit at me!
I felt someone's warm hock and it made me feel
like I was drooling bad breath mucus
it landed on my lips
I wipe it off with the sleeve of my cardigan
then I lunged for him!
but I got pummeled by his wolf pack of friends
I got spit on, two blackened eyes and I don't even
know why
I also wonder why no one tried to help me
I limp to science bleeding from my nostrils and my
eyes are closing forming purple circles
the teacher calls the guidance counselor, the counselor
called my mother, my mother came over
son who did this to you?
I say the usual, I didn't see, they attacked from
the back
she took me to the hospital and I leave with a cane
and some ice packs
dad comes home, sees my condition and he's furious
he wants to kick some ass
son who did this to you?
again I can't tell the truth
the doc said I couldn't go to school for a
few days so I can recupe
a few days passed and I've recuped

on one of my days off, while mom and dad
was working
the bridge of my nose still hurting
I got an idea
I said I know a way that this won't ever happen to
me again
I go to the pawn shop and purchase two hocked glocks
with bullets by the box
this bullying is gonna stop!
I gotta hide what I just bought,
what better way than my school's Jan sport
the next day, it's back to school time
everything at home is the same
if only they could read my mind
I get dressed as always, mom dropped me off like always
now I'm an armed kid walking school hallways

now back to the top......

damn there they go again and math class just ended
the corridor is filled with students, as I see their movement
they're approaching
before they can push me and punch me
I go into my knapsack and pull out my two new
gats
and start shooting as something came over me
the school is in chaos
cell phones are dialing 911
a bullied student is wreaking havoc
today I'm not having it
he picks off each wolf from the pack
they was running for their life before being shot
in the back
pop, pop, pop, pop, pop
I don't stop until both pistols remained cocked
back
I now wear the evil grin
the other students and the teachers were scared
to approach me

I run out the school with the two empty guns in
my hands
I run right into the man...
freeze, put the guns down..
I don't, as the cops squeeze, blam blam blam
he's down, he's down, get the medics! I never make it...
I go from an innocent kid being bullied to a killer being
killed

this is now the action and reaction of being bullied

Forgiveness

would it ever be possible?
would I ever be forgiven about the past and
how I was living?
I'm just wondering if all those I seek forgiveness
from are listening
I'm sorry
some saw me as a way out of poverty when I was trying
to find my own way out so they followed me
I was moving forward with so much momentum and
didn't realize I became such an icon
I was doing wrong trying to live right
all I got was misery
stitches and scars from the drug fights
I was lucky
a lot of the ones that were following me, following
others are now deceased and that kills me
I live with regret constantly reminiscing
it's so hard to forget
I don't want to forget faces
just all the dark traces
the footprints of darkness where death took place
I can't turn back the hands of time
I can't change the reaction of our actions
but I can change the future so none of the things
from the past continue to happen...

Child Abuse

I'm being held captive
I've been held here for years
my yells and cries for freedom are not heard
I'm weak due to hunger
I guess my captors only have enough to feed
the voices I hear through
the door and not me
as I smell the aroma of my favorite dish I go ballistic
I try to scratch my way out the door
to no prevail, my fingertips bleed because
I lost all my nails
my eyes are super sensitive to the light
so I only get about 15 minutes for recreation
at night
when all the voices I hear are out of sight
except for those two, my captors
they brillo bathe me
they wipe away a layer of epidermis
because they feel I am filthy
it's been some time since I have eaten
grains of rice feel like shards of glass
cutting at my throat causing internal bleeding
I gag on water, as if I'm drowning so when I do drink,
I sip it
them withholding food and me not able to eat has me
looking and feeling malnourished
whip...... whip..... I get beaten
because of how slowly I been eating
then sent back to the dark dungeon like some
crazed heathen
I fall into fetal and fall fast to sleep....
a daily routine..
in the morning I hear those voices of fun
and laughter
I wish I can play with my brothers and sisters...
I just don't think that's ever going to be ok with my mother
and father's captors

A Survivor

people used to tell me "Al, you make wrong decisions"
like if there was options to a life of the forsaken
I was just following the blueprint of blood red pavement
of bereavement in housing tenements
when I tore through the womb of my momma causing
vaginal trauma
in 1971, do you think my plans was to succumb to the
dangerous streets?
what did I know about narcotics?
what did I know about being an illegal pharmacist?
what did I know about firearms and ballistics?

NOTHING!

I went from being premature, to a juvenile, to a criminal
growing up in poverty and mimicking the pusher selling
what burns in stems or what filled needles before self
inflicted injections
ghetto life misery sedatives that sedated our own relatives
I was 12 mixing pyrex pots in New York City the melting pot
on lucrative spots
instead of playing with Hasbro I wanted my own blocks
and lobbies
which is the reason why I got a bullet in my chest and dime
size burn marks on my body
you think mommies want this for the baby she protected
for months in her body?
we didn't even want to live this way, were born pure, but
poor
so our innocence quickly strayed away
the streets will misguide ya
I'm glad to say I am a survivor

Just Not My Eyes

I signed my license as a donor
use my heart, use my lungs, use all of my anatomy
any part of me
if you could cut my legs and give them to a person with
prosthetics legs to help make them walk and run perfect
so be it
give my arms and hands to the ones that can't touch
so they can feel
give an abused person my heart so they can defend
themselves with the soul of a boriquen Indian warrior
then they'll have the strength to overcome their oppressors
use my mind for the mentally handicap
just please do not use my eyes... I forbid that!
what my two eyes have recorded inside would cause the
average person to commit suicide
we're born to live...
looking through my eyes it would look like if I was born
to die
death was around so much
I had breakfast with the devil and with the reaper I ate brunch
with both I had dinner
people died morning, noon, and night
more in the summer than winter because hell's flames didn't
burn properly in lower degrees
I saw family tree branches fall with the leaves
an entire generation incinerated
grand kids calling grandma and grandpa, mommy and daddy
because they lost mommy and daddy
I viewed many viewings
I saw faces of distress
tears dripping from under shades
no make-up looking a mess
black suits, black dress
two belts
four men lowering those viewed to rest
those goodbyes look like horrible departures
mental torture like the thorns they placed on the head of

my brother
I saw stains that were once brains till it got brushed into
the ground
I saw hell on earth
I've seen preemies dying prematurely after being birthed...
so please use all of me
just not my eyes

A Mother's Fear

Moms is pushing for life
literally, she was pushing out mines
seven months carrying me around in her swollen belly
its time
she's on a hospital gurney ready to deliver her premature baby
her hands grasping the bed rails firmly, heavy breathing,
yelling and screaming, my head, my body, my feet
I take my first breaths of air
I whimper the world is new to me
my eyes have yet to open
I'm scared
umbilical cord cut, placenta all in my hair
they clean and then wrap me up to remain warm
placed me in my momma's arms
she beautifully stares at her newborn
she cries tears of love for the baby that was sent to her
from above

mom and dad took well care of the second child they had
they have already experienced raising their previous son
my older brother
ten years later they have another one
my little brother
two years later daddy dies
this is the point in time when mom really suffered

my little brother barely got to even know his father
my older brother was out trying to figure out what the
world had to offer
we was down on our luck
the projects didn't grow flowers
there was no four leaf clovers
moms sitting on the sofa feeling life was over
housing banging on the door, rent is three months past due
daddy was the bread winner, he's gone
what are we to do?

we was facing eviction
I was so close to going to military school but with daddy
dying that became fiction

I started to break curfew, started skipping school
started learning how to gamble and hustle
constantly in some trouble trying to pop poverty's bubble
the way so many tried and died
ghetto suicide

Momma found out I was selling drugs
it destroyed her
hugs became slaps
came home one day after days away and my clothes
were packed
there was no space for a project lobby loiterer
me a drug seller, she wasn't ok with
I walked off into the sunset at fifteen to become rich
and famous

at fifteen, I was locked up
at sixteen, I was shot twice
at eighteen, I was the most popular guy on the block

me getting shot and killed or life in prison was my
mother's fear
thank god I made it out so momma doesn't shed another
tear

Trapped

trapped in a body of a kid was a mind of a man
I was far too advanced
all my skills and senses were enhanced
I heard things different, I saw things different
I did things different because I was different
Yeah, my blood is blue and when it touches air,
it turns red
yeah, my blood is blue and leaked out red
I survived while most are dead
older guys dealt with off track betting
I was thinking money like them
I was in the trap peddling
passing bombs like a marathon
I was doing hand to hand no, not passing
the baton
I was running fast like Lewis and Johnson
pushing the Johnson & Johnson
I was a problem and I had problems
I was trying to feed my family and get moms out
of housing and I did!
after moms bid, we got evicted
imagine that, I felt so bad
we traveled the Bronx like nomads
no furniture, just a few bags
some pots and pans, forks and spoons
renting one bedrooms for a family of six
most places was worse than the bricks
I hustled harder, I was in knee deep now
I'm in even farther
I was being consumed by the streets just like my father
(Pause) our fathers
they are in heaven
I couldn't become him so I did "me"
you know my vision of happiness was chasing
money
to me, life had had no meaning without dealing with
things monetary

the streets was my love thang
I had dollar signs in my pituitary
I rolled myself up in a condom and sexed her daily
I was a crack baby
nah, moms wasn't getting high
I was serenaded by Ms Street's lullaby
she was a cradle snatcher
instead of "go to sleep, go to sleep my little baby"
the song she sang me was "come with me, come with me"
she spoke to me in trance like frequencies
I cried out for love
the streets gave me lust
for the "in god we trust"
most went back to ashes and dust
when the guns bust and the smoke clears
the streets disintegrated my peers
those were the bad years
after the cars, the glitz, the glamour,
the arm and hammer
that cake batter
I had to use my smarts, and my senses to
reinvent myself
realize my worth
I put my mind to work
then…
Infinite The Poet was birthed!

Time

three decades caught up in the street life facade
10,950 days
ducking narcotics, and evading gun spray
sometimes it was unavoidable
it's the inevitable, I'm never alone
I walk with a slug till this day
casualties from war occurred just by walking to
the corner store
it's absurd, our ghetto blocks pack plots by
the herd
from rat-tat-tat, kick the can
it went to brat-brat-brat, my homies kicked the can
dudes I went shopping with at Jew man and hosiery
are now symbolized by a card and rosary beads
I saw them bleed, they saw me grieve
I've seen things most won't believe
just one of my harsh days will equal someone else's
life of insanity
like fingers in holes in bodies to stop leaking anatomy
like seeing the faces of mommy, daddy, brothers and sisters
after telling them the occurrences of "today" shortened their
family
I bleed non-fiction on conditions of lost or forgotten children
I be them!
just in the form of a grown man with wisdom
so I wise the dumb with mathematical precision
a little of my one and two so you could understand
I dig deep to write with emotion
my pen cries an ocean
I already cried a river when dad never made it to dinner
that was 28 years ago
that and the consequences of the game cause this hemoglobin
to flow
I write mass-contusions to get into the head of the masses of
children and adults still caught up in the confusion of coke and
heroin, selling and abusing
I have a glossary of phlebotomy

I write about life's irony I spit red/white blood cells,
it hits hard, that's the iron me
these are words from a renegade youth with a street life
pedigree of OG
because most just didn't get to live as long as me
my wings were earned before I earned wings I
flew away
a lot that flocked with me, got wings clipped or live life in
pelican's bay
an hour of natural light a day due to the street life mixed
with poverty and kids dropping out of school
our ideas of being rich were uneducated guesses, ghetto
hypothesis

The Darkness

while living in the dark I always saw a light
I tried to follow it but it felt like it was unreachable
like if the light for an urban New York kid wasn't allowed
so I would stop the chase and reenter the shroud
thirteen project buildings whose majority was minority
hungry crowds permanently living under a destructive cloud
drugs, guns, love?
there was none when it came to pain and hurt, we had a surplus
that was the dark clouds purpose
its thunder is ferocious, its rain is murderous, its
wake is phosphorus

I wanted to escape the darkness so I tried chasing
the light
I jumped over trial and tribulations like an Olympic
hurdler
every time I got closer it seemed like it moved further
each time I ran longer I was telling myself while living in
despair, gasping for air
soon I'll reach that light to help my widowed mother, older
and little brothers

dark clouds kept dropping red rain
I got tired of the agony and have to save my family
I couldn't continue to view this life as the norm
I gathered the courage to run through the storm
I ran and ran
I'm gonna catch up to the light
I'm running with all my stamina and might
I pass out running away from that destructive life chasing
better days for me and mine

I awaken to the sounds of birds chirping
the sounds of fun and laughter
my eyes squint from the brightness cause I'm in
the light!
I found the sunshine to live happily ever after

Da Bronx

you can hear advertisement for jumbos next to the advertisement
tempo before random shots blow
that's how you know you're in the Bx borough
po po comes down the block, you hear bajando
they go up the block, you hear subiendo
they leave, you hear tato
that means everything's a go but if they jump out everybody blows
dryers are bars on our window
the pavement you walk on is half concrete half gum
kids flipping on pissy mattresses on curbs is not absurd you reached the slums
chains sway from bars where swings once swung
you can only teeter not totter because hustlers cut the wood to make the winter drug spot hotter
it became ghetto lumber
dogs sipping from broken fountains leaking water
mobile basketball courts are in the middle of the street obstructing traffic
the free throw line was behind a car that been stripped
you know when you're in the Bronx when you walk through a black or spanish community
get randomly frisked because we fit the profiling descript perfectly because you're black and spanish
museums of natural history are schools
high powered blast from fire hydrants are pools
at night lobbies become clubs
parks become pubs and opened air stores for drugs
no prescript needed
just a 20 or 10 dollar bill, a stem, needle or Dutch to get inebriated
our dads drive papi cabs if you need to get to the boulevard in a hurry
just listen for the beeping horns and "story story"
and if your old school when u got there
you would of seen one of New York's last trollies

Perdon Madre Mia (Forgive Me Mom)

my mom, without her there would be no me
she's the alpha queen
the most dominant woman on this planet to me
my mom is there for me through thick and thin
through the good and through sins
and never left my side no matter the condition
I know I caused my mom a lot of pain and suffering
cause of the game and me hustling
I wouldn't stop cause I was so selfish
you saw the child to whom you gave birth living less
than his worth
I know it ate you up every day to see it
I continued that life for years with disregard to momma's
eyes filled with tears
I thought it was bettering the family
even though mom didn't accept it and would always
contest it
I never dreamt of her getting arrested and having a
criminal record
mom, when you was gone, I took the best care of your
youngest children
they didn't understand the position we was in with the
bureau of child welfare looking for them
and that their moms, dad and older brother was in prison
I didn't mean to do it but my actions were influenced by the
environment I lived in
my mother gets out of jail to deal with another problem
the city no longer wants us to live in housing so we got evicted
all this has happened just as my mom warned and predicted
mom, you will never know how sorry I am cause I did not
listen
and for my actions I sent you, Tone and Sid to prison

Build and destroy

I went to temples and mosque when I was younger
my dad used to take me
he placed me on the shoulders of Muhammad Ali.
zuit suits with hair brushed to the side burnt with lye
can't forget the bow tie
the bean soup and pie
I still remember his degrees in my head
they stick mathematics, alphabets, 12 jewels, 1- 14 and 1- 36
Do you over stand me?
my attribute to god is infinite
Gods cipher is divine
no yellow number five
lecithin and gelatin, unhealthy swine
I learned about Elijah, Farrakhan, Malcolm, Marcus
and our brother Jesus all at the same time
imagine my state of mind
like Martin, I have this dream
before it comes true boom another obstacle
levees, tornadoes, eruptions from volcanoes,
tsunamis, quakes, air craft carriers and subs
my peoples still drowning in blood
our peoples are still in need not able to rise up and live out the true reason of our creed
my mountain tops are ghetto blocks
I speak wisdom to loosen the noose around the neck of our young children
I was alive in the last recession
awake in today's oppression, a deep depression
face to face is poor people interrogation
drugs still enter our borders used by our sons and daughters
we killed each other for what we sold
another form of population control

My Infinite Symbol

I stood in the shadows of the ones before me
I studied the path of the once mighty
I rolled with the strongest
the ones that were street savvy
for richer or poorer we married the streets
lost a lot of peeps for domestic violence
not man beating woman, this bitch beat men
I saw many friends covered in white sheets after this
domestic violence transcends
first audio then video, gun shots then filming where
the body drops
cops search for the perps that just made the John Doe the
"late" another episode on the first 48
I proceeded with caution as a kid
the streets tried to give me an abortion in the form of
other reckless kids trying to push back my wig
if it wasn't for Edgar Morales taking one in his neck
I might not of lived
while most was listening to Bell, Biv and Devoe
I was caught up with that shit that had peeps scratchin
elbows with an ill flow
that stuff was poison, like ivy
had fiends scratching their body
no bushes around, this happened in project lobbies
my dreams of blowing up exploded
disintegrated my men to gas in the atmosphere
some get stuck in the thermosphere
I escaped liked a molecule that had enough velocity
to exit the exosphere
that's why if you look up to the sky, you'll see the
infinite sign appear

Driving Out Of Poverty

our house was packed
heads from the living room to the back
of our two bedroom
it was my immediate family and we made
room for relatives immediately
we never denied food or shelter to a family
member
it's been like this for as far as I can remember
love was in a lot of boxes, which lined walls
sometimes blocked doors
we loved material things
everything we bought and didn't want got
packed
then stacked, then forgotten about
it was crowded, I loved to get out of it
so I would always hope any drive out of
poverty that I would be invited

the car I would be in would time travel from a
littered road, graffiti walls, from every block liquor
stores
from the sound of macks, techs, and 44 rounds
and from the shells that fall to the floor and sparkle
like glass
from the investigating
from the covering of the brass that
shines like glass
being covered by numerals
from casket to dirt covered funerals
from the advertisement of the boy and girl and I
don't mean children
I mean the uppers and downers
the sniff or the tap on the arm main vein hit
snorting and shooting
this is still my neighborhood I'm seeing but as the car keeps
moving
I start to see different sceneries

we jump on I- 95, 65
15 minutes later in any direction things got better
you could actually read the signs
the roads are paved with white lines
no advertisements of drugs
no sight of crime
home away from home everyone looks happy
things are fine and dandy

I saw spanish and black men with suits
I assumed they were rich
in the hood you don't see that often unless you had a
court date or became the "late" laying in a coffin
I saw shiny new vehicles, leather interior
brand new paint jobs looking like colorful
mirrors
everyone greets each other
how do you do Mr. Frasier, afternoon Mr. Rivera unity
everyone knows each other
a close knit community
they look out for their neighborhood
they do their own security
the local store might not have quarter water
but when you go get poland spring for a dollar
the owner's not following you all over
no one's rushing you to buy
they're not judgmental of my skin color with darker dye

the driver says, it's time to go back home
trips over, I ask why?
back on I-95, 65
I soak in the scenery
I wouldn't even blink my eyes
then... unreadable signs
dirt and grime
graffiti,
entrepreneurs of nickel and dime crimes
I'm back home
the travel ended

I release a sad sigh..

now I'm back where it started in the projects
on my sofa with my cousins and my brothers
telling me to move over reality
I can't wait for my next ride to travel out of poverty

The Ghetto Poetical Alto

I dealt with death
what was being sold was murder
manufactured cain with poland spring
and a lil yellow box of arm and hammer
took my metal clothing hangers to reach
in the pyrex to whip up a gooey batter
let out some hot, let in some cold, solid rock
the best traffickers got it sold
look outs looking out, pitchers pitching
managers patrolling peeping the scenery
bosses count stacks while blazing the
greenery
connects waiting daily to feed me
nothing was stopping me
fuck the world
life to me was a huge everyday orgy
I was tricking, money was disappearing and
reappearing like a magician
a cocaine politician
polly-o was my slogan
lots of mozzarella for what I cooked over the oven
lots of cheddar fogettaboutit like goodfellas
a lot of gwop for the different color tops of vials
filled with rocks
we competed with the competition
till there was no more competitors
mission completed
had to come see us if that thing
was needed
we were social misfits
so we socialized with the optimistic
we might die we might live
dimes nicks treys, white powder crime
the bad ole days, we did bad all day
things would get worse for the thirst of cash
the guns started to blast
I know firsthand

a few slugs hit my ass and some hit my men as well
they would have this same story to tell but they passed
I cried a farewell
the streets said oh well because of the temptation
to rise out of poverty illegally
almost my entire team fell
we went from hood stars to the world is mine scars
now we're a few old stars with puncture or bullet scars
mental scars, mental bars conflicting with the vision of the 3rd eye
mental incarceration
man has 7 ounces of brain
I do so much thinking I think I thought a few grams to oblivion
I'm 40, my experiences are those of a senior citizen an old timer
because of ghetto grammar and the devils batter
its bringing me closer to catching Alzheimer's avenues and streets that brought in revenue
most likely cause the death of you
I've seen some respiratory vegetables
they would never look at me again
that's so incredible
it wasn't acceptable but there's nothing to do when God's coming for you
I didn't have the power to resuscitate sorry men
I couldn't rescue you but you know what?
because of you, I've got a powerful tool
the tool of prose/ spoken word to educate our youth

A Slave

a walk through my old neighborhood
I see a lot of people I used to see doing the same old thing
on the same corners, selling rock, getting locked up
and spending money on lawyers
undercover police sending confidential informants to silently
infiltrate drug infested corners
females still running the blade and guys still falling into the
trap
for blocks they consider theirs
they bust their gats
old timers still on the block doing the same old thing
catching Alzheimer's while the young guys sling and dream
of becoming the next big timers
there's cameras on every building in the stairs,
elevators and lobby
watch what you do in the open
big brother is invading peoples' privacy
I see girls that I knew when they was kids having kids
all grown now
their kids followed the same cycle now
this girl is a grandma
our name was "kunta" but we lived like "toby"
other than ourselves cause I did what they taught me
instead of sticking to my "roots"
I was replanted with evil seeds
I can't recant my evil deeds
they were implanted and embedded in my mind
mental swine
I wasn't on hallucinogens but must of been hallucinating
when I was propositioned to sell my soul to cope with
the position I was in
poverty stricken and 1 parent missing
nothing worked in my favor so I signed the
devils waiver became hell's waiter
lived life fast
left a trail of flame for those following my path
you would have to walk through fire for the things

I desired
or maybe you would walk away when you feel the
intense heat before you get smothered
in the smoke for trying to make ends meet

Dangerous Blocks

dangerous blocks
9 millies, 44's, 5's
buck shots
choppers bustin off the back of choppers
like the hell's angels, corrupt cops
rocks and crack pipes
la marqueta where murders shop
where men murderers get shot by murderesses
can't trust cute faces in dresses
they could be a gangster's mistress
misses married to the married to the street's
misters
hope I didn't confuse you
I'm painting a picture of men and women leaving you
dangerous blocks where bad boys move in silence
they throw up signs like sign language
pulled triggers quietly, kept their guns silenced
get caught they're mute
they bring in interpreters
they sign we want lawyers
they don't speak
dead men don't talk
after trial they walk
they once again stalk the streets of New York
dangerous blocks, where goons, pushers
and thugs roam
the females were medusas
they seduce ya
all four creatures have the some plot
six foot deep spots with head stones made of marbleized rock
this is the welcoming committee in back avenues and streets of
the city
the only ones that survive are the witty
any other sub phyla gets thrown in the fire with no pity
dangerous blocks turn innocent people evil
home invaders invade their neighbors
a neighbor foils the plot

doesn't have a license for a gun but to protect his family
he takes random shots
an invader drops
the innocent homeowner calls the 911
investigation from cops begin
the invader lives but gets 10 years
the homeowner gets taken down along with
him
he gets acquitted for the attempted murder
it was self defense but he gets charged for the
illegal gun
gets a few years because of someone else's
nonsense
there goes an innocent mans innocence
he went from protecting his family to getting
jail visits from his family

The Result Of A Gun Shot

pop, pop, pop
impact
Al is hit, Al is hit...
I'm asleep with my eyes opened wide....
my blood leaks from parts of my body with
new openings...
I pass time....
my body feels dead... I have a conscious mind....
I close my eyes....
I awaken to the sound that the gurney and hospital doors
are making....
I look up to see this man and woman sweating
sprinting as if they're pushing a bob sled...
what's his status?....
a hesitation....
he just flat lined on the last turn....
doc starts chest compressions....
beep, beep, beep, beep....
I have a heartbeat again ...
x-ray after x-ray....
slicing and cutting...
stench of burning arteries...
I'm awake but can't feel a thing....
did you guys make an ID?...
nurse comes in hysterical....
yes.. he's only 16...
hurry call his mother, we need him to see her..
mom comes in, grabs my hand and prays....
so the lord came and took over the operating
procedure...
I was too young to die....

Mr. Street!

yup you made me, I won't lie
dapper d, bells fashion
I let the 5 lace me in leather
I'm the don
was an eighties crack baby
nope, moms wasn't smoking
you had me at twelve tailor made
I loved New York
you had me selling crack while sketching
on the floor
a skelzzy board with chalk
then you had me drawing guns to defend
our trap
I'm no hypocrite Mr. Street you were inconsiderate
I understand you got me and mommy out
of poverty
hustlers are a majority of the minorities
16 with a back pack full of crack in port
authority or passing through customs at JFK
with coke wrapped in plastic
swallowed there in my anatomy from the
block to miami
shit them out
now these Bx streets help feed another
family

let me tell you what you did to me
for giving me fast money, fast honeys, fast cars
you gave me mental scars, physical scars
I'm scarred
I tell my kids my bullet holes are burns
I hear gun shots and start to dial a friend who's
been dead for years
I'll say about ten
It's that it still seems like yesterday
when bullets spray we made sure we're ok
I never erased their numbers

I scroll through them everyday saying grace
remembering their face hoping I press send
and just for a few seconds I can hear their voice
on the other end
every time I pass St. Raymond's Cemetery in the
Bronx
I do the sign of the cross for all the people I lost
I pay the toll crossing into Queens
I'm still signing the cross for members of
my team
imagine the toll it takes on me remembering them
I'm on the LI expressway
exit thirty now I finally finished crossing
so I say amen
if I reminisce on everyone that's gone
I would of said amen in the Hamptons

so yeah you made me!
you made me a product of your environment
Mr. Streets
but you know what?
me and you lost our chemistry
I no longer do housing chemistry
you should of finished me like you finished them
now with my voice echoing in the slums letting the ghetto
children know the streets are condemned
now it's time for us to bury you
the street life is dead

Ms. Streets

I'm a product from a hood environment
I was innocent until I was altered
I was forced to be married like some cultures
I married the streets
the pusher met me at the alter
the avenue preacher asked, do you promise
to hold these cracks to make you richer after
being poor?
Do you promise to pack a gat every time you leave
your project apartment door?
I couldn't say yes or no
this marriage is set up
I had no idea what was in store.....

I asked Mss Street, why do you want to
marry me?
I'm so young and poor
she says you have curfew
I want to give you freedom
you're poor
I am going to teach you things now at an early age on how
to get money so you can be a better husband
I say no curfew, more money?
don't stop now keep talking to me honey!

mom and Ms. Streets didn't like each other
they were familiar
my dad cheated with Ms. Street's mother
mom said I'm warning ya that family of women
is psychotic killers
I should of listened to mom since I was little
I felt stuck in the middle
my life was like an auction
moms was a low income receiver and Ms. Streets
was the highest bidder, I was sold

(In my auction voice)
red top, blue top ,pink top
I gather the buyers by advertising what I got
I became an auctioneer
do I hear three? three dollars?
do I hear five? five dollars?
do I hear ten? Twenty?
sold to the fragile looking, cheek protruding,
sick man and women in the back
the ones in the front in a shivering huddle
nodding
quickly kick the monkey
when I start the bidding for a bundle, the bundle is
fifty
I auctioned it off for seventy
I made twenty dollars p c instantly
Ms. Streets is teaching me.....

Ms. Streets showed me how to make money
she said she loved me
here take this, it will help you in a life threatening
crisis
always keep it on you for protection you not coming home
to me frightens me to even mention
out of all my ex's you're the best
what she gave me was a 9 millie and a vest
she loves me.......

mommas worried Ms. Street got the best of
me
I was young
cell phones have yet to come
so she beeped me "baby come home" she needed me
I run to the corner phone, call home to tell mom
"I'm ok"
she hears my voice and instantly cries frantically
she says you're going to be the death of me
she doesn't own you, I birthed you
you're my baby, she's my enemy

(Please deposit 5 cents for the next 2 minutes)
no more change, the phone hung up on me.....

I run back up, to Ms. Street...

I went to jail for Ms. Street
I sent moms to jail for Ms. Street
I sent my older brother to jail for Ms. Street
sent my two little brothers' father to jail for Ms. Street
you know what I got from Ms. Street?
she branded me for life
I got bullet scars on me, mental scars in me
she must of been practicing polygamy
she married my dad, all my young friends and me
she told me she was a widow
but not how many times and that she was the one
dating them on final calling time
I think I'll leave before she steals this soul of mine

I asked for a divorce, she asked, "why?"
she was defiant
I said I should of listened to my mother
Ms. Streets, you had me blinded
I hand her the papers, she didn't sign it
so I just walked out on her
that decision I'm glad I made it
it's been twelve years since me and that
bitch separated

A Serenade

the streets haunted me, as I was still in the cradle
mom gave me a half water, half formula bottle
I wanted Gerber cereal added but mom used her
last wic check
so cereal was subtracted
she would rub me as I wept
thats when the streets started serenading me
"oh little baby don't you cry", I looked at mama
her mouth wasn't moving
I look around wondering where that sound is coming from
it's so soothing
I keep hearing this voice that's singing echo from out the
window
I coo from the tempting melody
it faded as I rested my head on the pillow
I fall fast to sleep
it seemed like every time I cry, I would hear some type
of jingle
I'm now 10, it's been happening since I was little
"Mama, I need new school clothes and shoes"
"sorry Al, I don't have the money right now"
maybe in a month or two
I cried! then heard, " let me help you"
I said, "what?"
mom said, 'you heard me, I said in a month or two"
I still hear that voice talking to me
I was being tempted, I just didn't know it yet
the voice is serenaded to innocent poor kids in the projects
I'm now twelve, I'm tired of crying and at the same time my dad
was in the hospice dying
he died, I cried
as soon as I shed a tear that voice appeared ever so clear
"work for me I'll make you rich as can be, your father's gone,
your mom's living in poverty, have no fear follow me"
and I did!
the streets gave me cocaine
taught me to mix it with baking soda, a little water, add fire

cook it till an oily goo comes back
add some cold water from the tap
voila, the streets taught me how to cook crack
the streets said, "see don't cry, I got your back
but just in case I'm not around, here take this gat"
yay, I got money from selling crack
everyone's scared of me because I carry a gat
while hustling in the trap, I'm the man!
how dumb or was I just young and naive?
how could I be deceived into doing what the streets
told me to believe and what would help me?
drugs and guns just added to my grief
the fast life is brief
at fifteen, I was locked up and a year later, I was shot
four years later my apartment gets raided by tactical narcotic
team cops
the streets lied!!!!!!
they abandoned me, they hurt me, used me
I was preyed upon
I got to leave the streets but my serenaded peers
like me are gone!!!!!!

A Letter to My Dead Friends

I remember my letters used to start off saying,
"I hope when you receive this you're in the best
of health"
I guess I have to start it a little different
it starts with the sign of the cross
I can't write because you can't see so I'm going
to recite
I know you guys can hear me
I miss you guys!
I miss you guys dearly!
I pray, I ask the lord just to have you guys back another day
why I ask that?
my reason is because I don't think I got to tell them that I loved
them on their final day
I was probably caught up in the drug life
somehow as their blood leaked out as juveniles due to gun spray
at times, I break down because y'all are not
around me physically
I always wondered how life would be
if y'all were still with me so I dream
Bunca looks like bips
Orlando looks like junior
Eddie looks like little Eddie, I say like little Eddie
because big Eddie died at 17
Little Eddie is now in his 20's so he's older than his father just
like me
Edgar would look like papo
lil Edgar looks exactly him now
Blue would look like his dad minus the alcohol
Koko would look like Gwado
Ralphy and Skipper brothers in heaven
Ralphy would look like a blonde hair blue eyes version of
Jonathan
Skip looks the same just at peace, we just lost him
Chris would be a young version of Mr. Gresham
this is me guessing how I would look walking
another day with you guys

I want to let you guys know how life has changed
I found a way out from slabs and vials packed with cocaine
our story is helping others change their lives
writing is my new lane
no more street fame
people from the states, Japan, China, Africa, Australia, Indonesia, Europe, Latin America
now know Infinite the Poet's name with the lemniscate burning flames
that path we walked on, I no longer claim
I'm unpaving it, then repaving it with the 7 ounces of my brain!
I had to recite this pain to let you guys know you didn't die in vain.
I love yall !

Life In The Hood

we knocked on pipes for steam in the winter
laying cold at night on the same bed with a peeing little
brother or sister
mom or dad in the other room
I say mom or dad, it was rare you had them
both
I ate stale bread, it taste better as toast
when I wanted cereal I had to shake then pour
slow to make sure I don't digest a roach
had a rocking chair that didn't rock
a recliner that didn't recline
a clock that couldn't tell time
a vice gripped faucet
a yellow stained toilet
no funds for a fuse in the socket
we used foil to keep the light lit
paper for a peep hole
sheets for curtains covering windows
food stamps changed to money so mommy can get through the
month
last couple of days it would be local community
center breakfast and lunch
we figured we can skip dinner if we went to
sleep early
back at the community center in the a.m. 7:30
I watched tv shows I can relate to like "land of
the lost"
we were living like in a lost land or "gilligans island"
we was stranded like the SS minnow
we were confused to hear Mr. Rodger's Neighborhood
because he was saying what a beautiful day it was
I used to look out the window to see where he was
I wonder, what neighborhood?
It wasn't mine he was speaking of
all I see is abandoned cars full of people using drugs
it wasn't a beautiful day to me!

Al Carrasco, The Revolutionary

I am a slum/ghetto/urban visionary
on the contrary to what I've visioned
I thought I was losing my mind
really, life was building mines
being dealt the lowest cards and the hardest blows
a life of subliminal woes settling for less is something
I will forever oppose
I did a lot of bad
not because I wanted to but because bad was the only option I had
by any means to rise out of poverty I did anything necessary
I had a passion to overcome instead of to succumb
to society
a society of systems and authorities that plague
minorities
the streets built a monster like Frankenstein with the wits of
Einstein
the problem is, I was using strength instead of
smarts
I was born with a lion heart
I used strength to rise to the highest plateau in the streets
I peaked, while at the top, I looked at the havoc
underneath
pain, destruction, misery, desolation, deception
the youngins were trying to follow a path I
mistakenly left them
this here is my road to redemption
I'm using my smarts to give strength
climbed down the plateau of today
back down to yesterday to show a different way
interception…poetic intervention
I'm showing a detour from body parts splattered
on floors
coroners and morgues
murals on project walls
I'm saving people from night time raids and early
morning graves

with my words, I'm trying to correct all the wrong
that was made
by shedding light on the dark days
I want all my people to keep hustling, just not drugs
follow my lead or join me
make lost men creme de la crem
I voluntarily speak opportunity to the needy
the needy needs me like I needed somebody to guide me
remember my name, I will make change
when I die, I will be known, as Al Carrasco, Infinite
the Poet, the ghetto revolutionary

White Girl

My ex-girl umm, umm she was fine
I did things I normally wouldn't do but I did
them for you
so fine pure white
her addiction is so wrong but at the same time
she made me right
we had this long abusive relationship
I didn't hit her although she was killing me softly
I sold her for a fee, she was ok with that
she said save your money and buy more of me
I know, I know she's a bitch for using me
but I was in love
she paid my bills, so what my blood spilled
as soon as I would recoup, like a fool I ran back to you
my white girl!
she sexed me daily, a cold lover
I didn't realize she was fucking a brother
I adored her the way she came, sometimes she liked
to be made up
so I added lipstick and foundation on her face
now she's in alter ego mode, I call her bass
when she's like this, she wears assorted colored caps
it's trendy when I vend her to nickel and dime
vendors
I wasn't pimping, she was pimping me,
it was costly
I got the courage to leave that hoe, it was time to
let her go
I no longer have her but I have the scars to forever
remember her name
bye, deuces, to Ms. Cocaine!

Dad, Can I Ask You A Question?

dad, can I ask you a question?
sure son, you may ask me anything
dad, I went over to a friend's house to eat, after dinner
we sat on the sofa to relax our food and rest our feet
while resting we got into a conversation about the streets
guns, drugs, and jail
how do people get caught up?
that's like the ultimate fail
his dad heard us talking, thought the conversation was interesting
he says boys, let me tell you a story about my friend....

guys, when I was young I had nothing
my parents were from the West Indies, Antigua
we moved here to the South Bronx in the 70's into
Castle Hill projects
to me a new life began, but my accent was thick
I really had no friends until I met him
we talked...he understood everything I said
I didn't have to tell him "yer ears na go tru ya head?"
so I shook his hand and introduced myself instead
his parents were from Puerto Rico
they was just as broke as us!
instantly we clicked
our mothers and fathers took us in like family
we was kids
we had no worries for money ....

he became my closest friend
he came to my house and ate dumplings with tails
of ox
Uncle Ben's seasoning and rice out the box
with our tongues we washed the plates clean
then it's off to his house, it's dinner time there as well
Carolina rice, beans with stewed beef
oh how I loved that smell
his dad was an air force veteran

my dad got a job a few years after we settled in
we was barely making it
we needed help so our mothers were welfare
reciprocated.....

he was so innocent, quiet, but militant
his dad had him that way
1984 came, the era of crack cocaine
also the year when his dad past away
after that year, for him, things wouldn't be the same
at fifteen, he got locked up for a gun
at sixteen, he got shot twice, I almost lost my friend
his mom almost lost her son
the streets were triph for him in his new life
he got caught up in the illegal curriculum
by the nineties, everybody knew him
but I knew him better than everyone else
he was a good guy stuck between a rock and a hard place
trying to increase his family's wealth
living at a fast pace....

 what happened to him?

it took him twenty years, plenty peers, many tears
incarcerated nights locked down days
he reappeared, he just walked away

what saved him?

the birth of his first son! His son's name is Aaron
wow that's my name the kid says!

whats your father's name?
Al he writes poetry
that's him! that's my friend!
that's my dad!
the conversation ends....

ok son, what's your question?

is it true?
and did you really leave that life for me?
I said, yeah son that was me, absolutely in layman's
love doesn't come with a price
so not raising you was something I wasn't going to sacrifice

thank you dad, I love you so much!

I say, thank you son you took me out of hell's clutch

These Two People

I haven't seen these two people for a long while
they are hearing and seeing me now
they are so proud of what I do instead of what I
was doing
they said they prayed for me since I was a youth
because at 12, I lived in modern day hell
but they said we saw something in you
I say thank you, do you like the stories I tell?
they say, I do
I say do you have time?
they say, I do
I say ok, here's one for you

I remember you guys saw me so caught up in
poverty
you went to work early, came home late
at both times you saw me in that NYCHA lobby
on a drug shift like it was a pharmacy
they didn't live in the projects
they lived across the street in some condos
but everyday they walked by, they saw the rush
people in line while their on line waiting for the
bus
they weren't scared of me, they used to warn me
walk to the bus slowly, preaching while talking to me
they tried to deter me but I was thirsty for money
I used to listen to their wisdom but my abdomen
kept telling me it's hungry
so right back to poverty-- no jobs, no help
just the streets calling me
my dreams of growing up with structure broke
dad's death caused the fracture
I never healed that's the cause of my life being a disaster
a young, serious kid, no fun and laughter
distributing the devil's batter
all it did was worsen the matter
these two people told me this then but I was a cub

growing up in a lion's den
I didn't pay attention
I just want to let you know I found fun and
laughter
I thank you both for your words
they probably saved my life!
I'm having this convo with a local pastor and his wife

Projects

from the start, day one we was being tested
they put a bunch of people in a usually 4 to 5 block radius called
the "projects"
no funds, no hope or help is how they contained us
they restrained us
if you can picture poverty
you're probably looking at us in a still shot or paused
frame
or just the lowest way of living flashing through your brain
that's the struggle we was in
door knocking for food to eat but in the street we killed each
other for the slightest idea of an opportunity to make ends meet
we got introduced to a plant warlord combined with drug lords
vs. the military
for this plant, they went to war for
the war was brought to our door
it was like the invasion of Normandy
you don't believe me
check out our local cemetery
it's full of project John Does and young project visionaries
whose revolution stopped revolving from crack, dilated pupils,
dope, head nods
what was that for?
people dying at the same rate as in Darfur
this happened in the 5 boroughs, NY, NY, big city of dreams
we bit the rotten apple and started feeding fiends
some feeders became fiends, some fiends became clean
same curriculum different players, in new teams
ghetto routines, repeated project miseries

A Kid's View

why does mommy and daddy always fight?
they love me and I love them but I always hear
them quarrel at night
in the day time, when I'm around I guess they tone
it down
today is different, daddy slapped and pushed mommy
to the ground
mama screams, "pack up your things and leave"
she no longer wanted the man she loved around because
he made her bleed
I can't believe daddy would hurt mom and actually pack
up and be gone
the fighting continued from a distance because mom
wasn't receiving any kind of assistance
anything we had, momma bought
why didn't daddy show us any kind of support?
time went by, I have my mom but my relationship
with dad is lost cause after about a year
mom filed for divorce
dad never taught me how to ride a bike
he never took the time to teach me how to defend
myself when a bully picked a fight
you know what?
maybe he did teach me, every time he beat mommy
I was watching
the next time I saw the bully, I attacked
I grabbed a fist full of hair, repeatedly knocking his
head on the wall
pieces of epidermis left on this concrete surface
from a gash
then he falls to the floor
as he yelled out the same thing mommy did
please stop, I'm sorry
like my father, I felt power so I hit him some
more
gash in head, a broken jaw, with a bruised body
then I realized, this is wrong

I grab and tell him I'm so sorry
the way he was bleeding was the exact reflection
on how daddy used to leave mommy
and it bothered me
how can a dad hurt a mom or a mom hurt a dad
I saw it
dad almost beat mom lifeless
I will never do what dad did ever again I promise
I'm just a kid growing up in a house of domestic
violence

The Crying River

ventilators, respirators
flesh and bone separators
broken vertebrae, broken families
funeral motorcades, crying eulogies
everyone sympathized when back to back death came
my brothers eulogize
we still franchised and monopolized
then again euthanized
we advertised our demise with disregards to tears
in mamas' eyes
the water continued to leak from mamas as they
weep after the reaper reaps
after the piper piped a death tune to a life so
ripe
I always ask why so soon?
young caterpillars killed as soon as they left the
cocoon
they didn't get to morph into butterflies
they morphed into angels with halos gracing the
skies
if I gather all the water and salt that fell
put it in one place, it will give you chills then shivers
I call it the "the crying river"
death water, no amoebas or protozoa formed by
the ducts of sorrow of parents
kids that will never see tomorrow

Good Times

we wished for good times
ya know a piece of the pie
it wasn't to be flamboyant
we wished to ride the wave of the rich
but drowned in the deadly current of the abyss
poverty and abandonment
most parents were absent
we reached out to be held but got pushed to the
depths of hell to where that one angel fell
counterfeit dreams to us was good money
stolen souls, brainless bodies, ghetto mummies,
hell's zombies
we looked for exit ways and guidance but we was
pointed in the other direction
when some saw the light, all we got was dark
reflections
incarceration and pressing buttons on hospital walls for more
morphine injections or funeral processions
we looked for sanctuary but found ourselves in the penitentiary
for chasing currency
relentlessly, looking for love, we looked at doves symbolizing
the ones we loved
we watched their soul fly away when the belts lowered
them that day
those days, many days, we had each other from born
day to mourn day, then lawn day, the day those doves
fly away
we got cheered on by doing negative actions
expendable gladiators in a game for assassins
we became pros at our craft
we were dr. hustlers
bullets entering skin were hood vaccinations
our street arbitration for hood violations
we was just too blind to see
we was drawing blood and getting blood
drawn
hood phlebotomy

no knowledge so we repeat his-tory
distorted family trees for destroying the leaves
that bloomed from the seed
widows in woe for what we wove
it was the only path given so we ran oblivious in
oblivion
felt like we was God's forgotten children
so we made spoiled decisions that left a lot of guys
rotten with a plot
and their face inscribed on rock so we will never
forget them

A 12 Year Old

at 12, I was in housing lobbies
chasing currency to get out of poverty
hoping the streets gave me clemency
I became a master of chemistry
it was my after school program
learning the measurement of soda to grams
I learned how a substance changes form
a powder to an oil to a solid
with water and fire
I kept my eye on it carefully while I
gyrated it
so excited on the outcome because it can
help my income
or help make the system thicken
it was just part of life where I was living
guidance for me was missing
because the lord took my dad away right before I decided to
make these bad decisions
I continued to do so, it was repetition
I learned about sales and competition
I learned about death and incarceration
courts and funeral arrangements
learned how life would be without those
that didn't make it
I traveled the world with my guys when we
were young, I was lucky
now I'm alone because they traveled back home
life is hard without them
if I wanna see their faces, I got to look through
old photo albums
but that's also hard
I start remembering the good times being around them
before they went back to God
so I trained myself not to get too close to people
I hold back emotions
I might love you but I won't say it

if I say I need you, might get taken away
I live like this every day so if you died today
I hoped not to wake up with sorrow tomorrow
that way of life was a bitch so I threw in the towel

Kumbaya My Lord

lights turned off, refrigerator is hot
7 or 8 people in a 1 bedroom, full of folding cots
at night it's so ever quiet
the only sounds you hear are the 7 or 8 bellies
howling a hunger riot
we placed pillows over bellies so the sound dampers
baby's wrapped in cloth, no income to afford pampers
heads of household pacing forwards and backwards
hoping tomorrow will end today's sorrows
and bring us fun and laughter

Kumbaya, my Lord, Kumbaya

I see him/her alone pushing a baby stroller
no friends, no family, no baby shower
an abused single mom or a divorced dad,
traveling the city to eat like modern day nomads
shelters in the winter, parks in the summer
community centers for a cold breakfast, a warm
lunch, and a mix of the two for dinner
one outfit wardrobes, broke,
down to their very last compound after pawning
what was around their necks and earlobes and after
everything that was worth something was sold

hear me crying my Lord

young kids with no direction looking in mirrors like vampires,
they saw no direction
caught up in the streets misconception
get burnt in the flames, spontaneous combustion to these ghetto
streets
it's easy to get sucked in
why would they want to live tomorrow knowing it's gonna be
déjà vu
someone adds to the murder rate
birthday cakes, then flower at a wake

they feel they have no reason to live so these bars I continue to give
the economy is screwed so death and drugs plague our city
it's destroying our people, faster than H I V

hear me crying my Lord, Kumbaya

1 rpg kills 30 plus marines, we lose a seal team
bring my brothers and sisters back from overseas
stop sending them home in coffins please
we killed Hussein, we killed Osama
why continue to fill the killed at war wall and bringing sorrow to military wives, husbands, and mothers?
young, veteran brave hearts protecting by killing and then getting killed
it's the same thing
equal but opposite reactions like ying and yang
when is this war gonna end?

OH, LORD, KUMBAYA

The System

I know the penal codes better than a legal aid
or an 18 b attorney
why is that?
all the knowledge I got from surviving the game
my first time at bat I could pass the l.s.a.t ,
I would probably graduate head of my class because what I
learned from a pyrex glass and how my homies kicked the can
amongst many
I learned 220 and 187 charges like the back of my hand for all
that transpired on drug infested land
for a powdery substance manufactured by man
if it wasn't for that cocoa leaf and guns there would be minimal
drug charges and a lot more parents enjoying their sons
a lot of kissing and hugging
a lot less dirt being dug and lot less mourning
a lot less would ofs and could ofs
we would actually see what the dead would of come
to be
mommies and daddies adding to the family tree instead of a
death anniversary
glossy eyes, teary cheeks
once on top of the world, now resting underneath
all my dead brothers I miss them
I wish death would of missed them
all my brothers locked down, I wish I can free them and give
them freedom
show them there's life once out THE SYSTEM

Action And Reaction

I wasn't stupid or dumb
I just grew up in the slums carrying packs of crack and different caliber guns around predicate felons
I was a peasant and that's a worker's ensemble
worked every day, that's why I was always in
trouble
in the trap, it's a must to stay strapped because in the school of hard knocks when you get left there's no coming back
so I went to class with a gat in my knapsack protecting my stash as I swept the Ave
I didn't want to be out there but those hunger pains I
remembered
so I stood out and ventured for legal tender illegally
if I would of gave up I would be giving up on my
family
I weathered the storm
I dodged bullets until I got hit a few times
I dodged the police till I got pinched a few times
I kept running streets with my mans, steel and contraband
I was trying to get money to feed mommy and get us out
of no man's land
I went through it all
from misdemeanors to homicide knocking on my
door
to me seeing my mans bleeding out on the floor
to moms cuffed being escorted out our apartment for what I was copping, chopping, packing, trapping
she told me that would happen
I always was prepared for the worst and prayed
for the best
putting my moms behind bars is still to this day
hard to digest

That Phone Call

it's 5 am, ring…ring
I pick up the telephone
it's a girlfriend of my friend screaming at a
high tone
I was half asleep
bed in my head and sand on my eyes
my heart sinks immediately from hearing
her cries
just from the sound of her sobs I knew my friend
is already or on his way to God
just won't be the first time I get" that phone call"
that I lost a friend of mine
I say, where are you?
she says laying over his body
I say, what happened?
she says someone shot my daddy
wtf am I gonna tell the family
I called the ambulance
in a few minutes they will be here I was told
they're taking so long his body is already cold
I think he's already dead, he's unresponsive
his last breathe was extensive
I tried chest compresses but the wounds in his
head
I could hear her over the phone trying to revive him,
she's relentless
I tell her stay on the phone with me while I jump in the car
and merk off to the crime scene
my adrenaline is pumping, my heart is skipping
like a murmur
racing to the spot where my friend just been murdered
I arrive and jump out the car
grab my friend's girl
I try to console her, she's crushed
to her, her world is over
I grab her hands from around my man's neck
as I pull her away, "no" is what she wept,

as I tried to control her
I get down to my knees, kiss his forehead
then pray for the dead
God, someone laid him down to sleep, I beg of you, his soul to keep and when I die please have him amongst the rest waiting for me at the pearly gates
then end it with an amen and God bless
I'm glad I got that prayer in
here come the coroners with a white sheet to cover him

Science

from the streets of hard knocks in the south part
of the Bronx
bagging contraband turning a project building to
Fort Knox
for revenue, we went to war like in Iraq
we were contras like in Iran
not talking about foreign land I'm talking about
in our own land
we were early drug era pilgrims
poor citizens in search of dividends
so we sold pills and powder by the grams
to some men we were pimps to them
they came to us with e pluribus
in exchange, they went on a date with lady heroin
death in bunches
holus bolus

we thought we were players
really we were pinch hitting for the devil
those that don't believe me come with me
bring a shovel to dig a few layers
I'll introduce you to my all star team
resuscitate them so they themselves can tell you
things ain't what they seemed for bling bling,
cash rules everything around me, c r e a m
we was hitting fly balls running from third to
the plate
getting blown down by an outfielder with an arm before
we slid to home plate, you're out
you just met fate
the umpire didn't make that call
it's the new players on the roster coming up to
create an empire in this game of hard balls and
cocaine wars

I soaked all this in my caramel pigmented skin
through my muscles through my veins

I know 1st hand about the game
about the pain, about the kites I write to homies
with no rights
so I grab the mic, I grip it, then I spit at it
I'm a spoken word fanatic
I use my God given gift to uplift the youth that's
gonna be future johns, or future inmates in maxy
max pris-ons
for chasing doe, death becomes you
I know it's cold, the projects were igloos, hustlers
were the ghetto eskimos

My Imagination

everyone's out of poverty
instead of famine everyone is fam and lend helping
hands
no one is better, no one's worse, everyone finds love
no guns burst, no blood thirst, everyone's wealthy,
all sick people become healthy
parents dying of old age
their children actually do the same
brothers not selling crack
sisters either(prostitution)
men caress women/men caress men
women kiss men/women kiss women
we all understand
no violence
no police brutality
no abortion
no divorce
no inmates
no control of population
more education
new legislations
no more war
biracial couples don't get looked at funny
causing their feelings to hide
african american fingers mixing with caucasian fingers
asian fingers mixing with spanish fingers
we all hold hands with pride
no gangs
no secret societies
no guilty till proven innocent
no hatred
a choice to worship who you please
a judgment free world
world of peace!

A Victim To Knowing The Ledge

I'm alive but I lost my dad and a lot of my guys
so I really didn't care for living
you see, I had hurt and pain, through my actions
my emotions were released
I was a beast and the streets was in my belly
I ate them up, they made me corrupt
every law enforcement officer knew I was always strapped with
thirty two life snuffers
and that I would snap if they tried to infiltrate my brothers with
under covers
it would be torture and hours to suffer so they kept their
distance from the bellaco resistance
I would of made a dog look like just a pest like Dennis
because I was the real menace of a poverty stricken society
I want to thank all of you for not judging me
I was a slave to the streets like a modern day Kunta Kinte
they made me other than myself,
whipped me, tortured me,
I kept a hold on me
Infinite, the Son of God
they couldn't break to call me Toby so I broke free
and now I'm telling you my slavery stories
again thank you for not judging me
there's a lot of Al's that won't make it to infinite so I made it my
business to use my linguistics to hit people on the head
like newtons law of physics, I spit rain when it's
warmer than thirty two degrees
I spit snow when it gets below
all year long I'm teaching the ledge so the masses know and can
try to get ahead before eternally being left behind
like the deaf, dumb, and blind
I heard and spoke and saw evil till I learned Knowledge,
wisdom, and understanding to awaken my people
I studied mathematics and the Bible like Brahma
Sutras to Hindus
let me teach

call me tikki tikki tempo-no sarembo-chari rbi ruchi-pip peri
pembo
my mouth is like a well, I let the water flow
could walk through a fiery furnace unscathed like
Shadrach Meshack and Abednego
I walked to hell and back, all I need was new shoes
I came back like how and owl views, 36 I see
I was brought here more than 379 years ago but I'm
only forty years old
I'm just a relative of one of the North American Native
Indians, do you understand my division?

After Nine Months

her belly was sliced from left to right, muscle guts,
a gruesome scene
I could actually see her spleen but then again, it was
so beautiful
blood uncontrollably pumping through veins and
arteries
there's a team of them, three people pulling and
cutting and burning
all I can do is watch
they drugged her but she's still awake grabbing my hand asking
me "please get this over with" for goodness sake
although she doesn't feel a thing
it started with one and two then three all the way up to thirty
rags of blood
I'm looking at this happen to the one I love,
things get crazy!
they are calling for a 4th person to come help with
the gore
my heart is pumping even though I saw this before
it just hurts to see what my wife had to endure
there's one thing I have to mention
she went through it to bring forth life after a C-section

Click Clack

click clack is the sound of hand to hand pulling
back a glock
you hear click clack, pull back, shooters shooting day and night
on my block
moms can't even shop
she works for robbers and fiends looking to
cop rock
click clack, click clack, like old school cabangers
click clack, click clack, OG's letting off bangers
because young G's are hungry for money so the old timers
they're not respecting as the OG's are expecting
then click clack, click clack the war begins
the war of sins, the war of dead presidents
slugs burning marks with darker pigmentation
if your light, lighter, if your dark
since I'm in between, my bullet holes and my skin
perfectly blend
tic toc like the machine monitoring my heart
that day, the day, D-day, click clack I got blown away
literally
two slugs hit me
my best friend Edgar Morales saved me before I was riddled
blue then red my arm my leg, my torso bled
the lord I begged, I saw the light, then returned to life
I made it through three nights watching good and evil
knights fighting for my rights
on the fourth day I'm back to living triph
same ole thing, living fast hopefully to build my stash before the
fat lady sings
she sings some unholy shit!
I think at a certain time she stuttered or her record skipped
all I heard for years was click clack, click clack, and
lost almost my entire clique

I Want To Be Just Like Him

he comes through the door the same way every day
eyes low from the indo
fitted cap to the side rocking a pelle pell
gores times, red monkeys or true religions

his little brother wants to be just like him

as he enters the house before he undressed he would take his
gun out
always with one in the chamber and would place it under the
cushions in the sofa

his little brother wants to be just like him

he would count his drug money while on the phone talking to
some hunny sipping henny with a cigar full of purple
this was the scene every day
right on the couch is where he stays comatose from the haze he
blazed

his little brother wants to be just like him

one day while big bro was asleep, little bro pushes
big bro over
reaches under the sofa and grabs the heat
puts on the fitted and the expensive jeans
looking in the mirror with his face all mean

his little brother wants to be just like him

lil bro looks at his reflection in the mirror
playing he says, what you want to do and pulled
the trigger
glass shatters all over, the bullet ricochets
now little brother mortally lays

his little brother wanted to be just like him!   the end

In Your Head

I try to write like a poetic neurologist
he's all up in your head like a psychologist
then control your mind like a psionisist
I'm getting this down to a science like a word
 play scientist thesis
then my pen moves with telekinesis
two physical eyes watching while the third controls motion
follow the pen rock, tic toc, tic toc , hypnosis
with my thoughts I can give thoughts to a fellow poet
with writers block my brain, plays a slide
I see mental pictures passing by
I choose one then jump inside
then it's calligraphy with mental telepathy
one more thing I must mention
I'm working on my PHD in ESP, extra sensory perception
open your mind

John Doe

John doe was the nickname of my friends when their reign
ended with no ID
that became the name on their toe, just temporarily till the phone
rings
then here come the crying to the mortuary
oh Lord, yes, that's my baby! cries their old lady
he was found in fetal position on the ground
cause of death? he got hit with two rounds
they went in and out, two holes to the back
and two through his forehead
no need for an autopsy, we know why he's dead and how he
died
no need to cut him
death certificate says, cause of death was two
projectiles to his cranium
no open casket to see the foreign materials
that fill those holes
the lasting effect of that is tragic
remembering a loved one with a forehead
filled with plastic
those memories still arise when I close my eyes
I see that horrific slide, still frames, the next picture
of the effects of a killer is just as horrid
as the first when the stills changed frames
they were all John Does till momma came and ID
with their real name

Stuck In The Middle

the cup she had in her hand became shards of
glass littering the floor
as soon as he walked through the door
she was aiming for his head
he ducked, the cup hits the wall
the arguments ensues
the name calling, the blame game
this is what it sounds like when doves cry?
these doves' cries are killing me inside
my whimpers are not heard
I silently shed tears
what I'm hearing and seeing is absurd
I'm stuck in the middle

It's a tug of war, I'm in the middle trying to pull the rope
of life together
they split!
she gets a lawyer, he gets a lawyer
now the war begins like Kramer vs. Kramer
She wants me, I want her
he wants me, I also want my daddy
what's happening to our family?
now I see them separately bi-weekly
why don't I have a say?
I want them both with me every night just in case I have
a bad dream
I can call out for either of the two, mommy
or daddy
didn't matter, as long as you came to my rescue
you both said that if I do good in school I can
have anything I want
I don't get anything lower than a ninety
the only things I'm asking for is my family,
mommy and daddy
the court grants mom custody, dad moves away
that crushed me
a few years pass, I start asking mommy sadly,

why you kicked out daddy?
she says when you get older I'll tell you why
my daddy met someone else, and she's having his baby
I hope they stay together for the future of my
sister or brother like a beautiful fairytale
so they don't feel like they're stuck in the middle
as well

The Mirror

when I look into the mirror I see a kid's dream
coming true, mine
I see a kid from the projects in this mirror who's going
to become a winner, me
I endured everything you can only imagine unless
you were me
poverty
death
treachery
a drug monopoly
lobby coke factory's
Infinite flier miles
from those constantly flying to the sky
the reflection in the mirror is this guy when he was
 a misguided kid, me
I was a breeze swept away by the wind, then by a
storm
then by a hurricane of destruction, corruption which caused
desolation, desertion
everyone is gone except a few tumbleweeds
the mirror is looking at one of them, me
I was so mad, kicked out, evicted,
my rent and the time it's due was always conflicted
me and mamma became nomads
this is why I see riches
I'm already used to living with rags, bullets burnt
and knife stabbed
the guy in the mirror is me
trial and tribulations I overcame to stare in this mirror
I held a gun in this mirror
I posed with dead men in this mirror
I counted a few million in front of this mirror
a killer killed the people I posed with and
counted a million within this mirror
it took forty years to be ok with this reflection I see
of me
we all do what we must, I pass no judgment

some people walked by when I was doing what
I must
then judge with that I wasn't content
my stomach cramps of hunger from me and my
mother and brothers gave me consent
so I took those packs to feed the Indians in my
tent
under these conditions the streets gave me
permission to survive
I am the man in the mirror that struggled to
stay alive

The Pain In My Pen

I have a lot of hurt to write about so the ink
eases my pain
releases the pressure off my brain
if not, my mind will clot like varicose veins
I flirted with death for money, power, and respect
let me explain in depth
after your reign in the drug game for fame
speeding through life like the third lane
there's gonna be some afflictions after " life"
conditions
like most left without a pot to piss in
big willy is what they should of been
same idea as the 1001 men that died before
them
ring o levio
the streets herded, placed a noose, and murdered my
people
we were hung man!
for hanging with our men in project lobbies twenty four hour
grinding, hand to handing, blam blaming
we were doe boys,
first name John, that's what the toe tag says when
they were gone, frozen calm
IV pricks on both arms
morgue window palm prints of distraught moms
I know I was most likely to be the one to pull them away that
day those finger prints were made
three days before they was laid, they covered their ears and got
shot in the heart trying not to hear the devil's serenade
but this fat lady sung, game over and their life had
just begun
a mother is son-less, a dad is son-less,
happened about 1 time every two years
a ghetto solstice, a family is in tears, a kid is in a casket
preserved with formaldehyde and embalming fluid
the world is so cold, kids killing kids at only seventeen years old

The Window

if I just sat by the window without looking out
if I would just sit there with my eyes closed I would
feel like I'm somewhere else
I can hear birds chirping, I can feel the sun shining
warmth on my body, it feels so good
I'm in a big house, enjoying the sun's beam
I'm in a lovely day dream
I hear footsteps of people walking while gossiping
and shopping
giggling and laughing while they're passing
I vision their faces with no worries at this moment
in meditation, so does mine
I hear cars whizzing by, driving into forever, I picture
me and them in that car together
I hear the sound of a low altitude plane
I picture my dame and me in first class with a rich man's
attitude,
" umm can you please give me a clean wine glass"
I can sit and take a deep breath of fresh cut grass imagining my
workers cultivating soil around my cement stoned walk path
industrial machines working, cutting my trees and trimming
bushes
so passersby can see my beautiful house when they
walk pass
I did it, I'm successful!
then I open my eyes and I'm looking out the window of my
housing vestibule

Thoughts

I have thoughts that I write on paper in many forms
rap spoken word or poetry like this piece
I think deeply, then write a Mona Lisa like " Infinite"
da Vinci
my pieces are eye catchers, talking about all three
I can break down my life in laymen terms so your
life could be sacrificed
so you don't learn what dead men already did
the consequences in the game are eternal bids
because of the crack holocaust, lives were lost in
abundance
this illegal substance destroyed our circumference at
the highest cost
young minorities being sentenced to life in the highest
courts
or six foot ditches with RIP tombstones for trophies
after dying to be living in the street life sport
I've seen guys that had it all at twenty
have absolutely nothing at all at forty
so in a twenty year stretch, they were the largest
now are average
all the material possessions are just mirages
so what was the basis?
I'm talking about the loss of life, criminal cases, all the glitz
and glamour, a young mind's mental oasis
anyone that spoke to me business wise saw the fire in
my eyes to capitalize
I was speaking to the wrong people
the pusher pushed me, a cooker showed me the recipe so the
streets was what interest me and that interest took the best
from me
so I've decided to climb back down from the very tip
of the tree
down this tree of destruction the many that climbed it died for
nothing and left families to suffer
so I'm uprooting this tree so I don't lose one more of my
brothers, and to save many others

Roaming

I roamed the streets like an urban cowboy,
pyrex pots, slabs, glassine bags
wouldn't get bagged because being an adolescent
was my best decoy
I was a c and d boy with that grade A
that's the real McCoy; fish, scale, or reina
don't matter I whipped it like avenna
150 b's of that boy g or bumble bee tuna daily
I'm an 80's baby
I had an obsession to getting money illegally from
coke leafs and poppy seeds feeding sick fiends
I was a sick fiend too
I was addicted to selling death on hell's avenues to make sure
my hand me down big bro jeans were stacked with revenue
I was a rebel relentlessly running rapidly rampantly in
an unreal reality
I took casualties casually because it constantly continued
consecutively
children causing chaos
guardians grieve grievance greatly at graves for losing
the child God gave
yep, this is a scenario from my dark days
none of us knew our worth, we lost a soldier in a
drug war but we gained more turf
this is my block, I want that block, let's take blocks
pop, pop, pop,
1 man, 2 men, 3 men, drop, now their blood is the
cream to our crop
I got tired of farming lost souls in the devil's thresholds
of crossover roads
so I write in codes for those living in the cold
it's a death arctic, red brick igloos, red water, blue blood
turned red when murdered
it was phlebotomy central slugs were needles in the streets
there's no IV so we just RIP

My Arrival

the world awaited for this urban poet like we wait for the cure of
aids
I have arrived, Infinite, the burning lemniscate
I got that project, ghetto, slum, drugs and guns fire in
my third eye
it transforms thought into sound so I manifest flame
on the game
the life, the get rich plight, commissary and kites
the transferring of bundles on conjugals for five
times the capital
I got the real life gift like Whoopi
I speak to those Swayzes then relay messages to mommy and
wifey Demis
Dr. Carrasco, I got a PHD
power to her dead people
the deceased talk to me and through me
I'm a ghost writer, a formaldehyde and embalming
fluent reciter
I put my heart into this when I attack most just murmur
my ink spills bloody murder like a dead kid's screaming
mother
horrific scriptures, as I paint mental pictures of a life so
sinister
I speak the reality a lot know but don't address verbally
well hell was my home
I'm not scared to preach because only God can judge
me and I know I'm being watched as I teach the juvys
adults too, the ones with kids and married having relations
with coke or heroin that's adultery and this is infinite poetry!

Guns

without my men I feel lost
wish I was there when the shit popped off
I'm sure in the enemy's mind they plotted making
sure I'm not around
the streets know I sense drama, word to my momma
I would of let off some rounds, dudes would of died
it just wouldn't be my homies bodies on the ground
lucky bastards
I was bred for war, shoulder strap, side arm and vest
when I walked out the door
I wasn't scared
I knew there was a chance I'll perish from existence
with the guns I bare
it was a part of that life
cold as ice was my steel touching my waistline to
prevent mine and others flat line
the thing is, I couldn't be everywhere at the same
time
I stood ready to roll, like two pits, being held facing off before
hitting after the flying kurz all you see was running kurs
then me chasing, busting, changing clips, I told my team
the scenario
keep strapped everywhere we go
they didn't rehearse so they got rears of a hearse
glued mouthed tuxedos, crossed hands holding a crucifix
at wakes is the worst
that shit plays over and over like a mental recorder
in my head,
that's on the spritz, always at the wrong time
I view funeral clips, my smiles get drowned out by frowns and
deep sighhhs
I fight the tears from falling from eyes but it's so hard cause I see
my guys
my guys died on a battlefield we called home so when I grab the
mic it's with mass appeal
like if it was blue steel with tracers, I hone in on my thoughts
and start lyrically attacking

I'm hurting so that life I'm dismantling you see I'm from the dark days of 1980 crime
that's when we started trapping after the era of break dancing and battle rapping
it became gun clapping, cooking coke to crack and
taj mahaj capping
we all carried joints, when someone killed someone
it was called scoring points, hustling is called the game
to those with evil thoughts murder was a sport
you didn't have to be in the league to play
all you'll be is an innocent "bystander" getting sprayed
I put my finger in stab wounds, I kissed the forehead
at wakes right next to the gun wounds
I pulled plugs with mothers, fathers, sons, and daughters
in the room
I keep seeing their distraught face after losing what came out mommas womb
you guys read and hear my words but you don't feel my pain!

It's So Hard

It's soooo harddddd toooo sayyyy goodbye to
yesterdayyy (In my boyz to men voice,)
yesterday my boys never got to be men
we were a bunch of cubs being mauled in a lion's den
ain't no sunshine when they're gone!
nope, it's been cloudy since they all left
it felt like every year our pack was one cub less
we're from a litter of death
trained to kill or be killed that's an urban skill
it's in our genes
no need to apply, if you're from where I'm from
you was born to die
why?
while we was babies, newborns
we witnessed poverty, moms couldn't eat so neither could we
there was no milk in the refrigerator or in the titties of our mothers
we were malnourished as we are rushed into an incubator
we grew up with the urgency to develop ways to make money with the government's assistance
the government lets a deadly substance into our existence that made profit
the coke epidemic, the crack era
in order to gain, we killed each other
now there's nothing we can do to stop it
an evil platform was made
a destructive foundation was laid
that's why being 40 in the slums is considered old age
the streets will always have drug dealing as an opportunity to make money
my words, the world must hear or there's going to be a lot of parents and kids wishing, like me, that their loved ones would still be here

Attempt To Assassinate My Character

the agony, the pain, after they pulled the trigger
this is what the bullet rang after the bang
as it twirls like little ballerina girls
it's searching for death, or the best thing next
like being a veggie or paraplegic
a wheelchair is detrimental when feet have no use for walking
on cement
or after being bullet riddled we become bed ridden with a tube
leading to a bag for us to piss and shit in
if we do walk again after the hot spirally object impacts, we may
walk with limps or with a set of crutches for amputated limbs
or a walker with tennis balls on the ends so we don't slip
burn marks mark our body from every bullet that left a clip
I tried to tattoo over what guns do
if you look you can't tell but if you touch you feel rugged
epidermis
where the bullets went through, they protrude
when its foggy or it rains, I got a slug by my lung, on these days
I feel the most pain
they say they spray with no names, not this day
I was the intended target to this lame he called a queen out her
name, so I came with the knuckle game like Mosley
next thing you know he pulled the trigger
the bullet rang after the bang
that sucker left me with 4 holes staggering into emergency
they started flushing me, lead poison testing me
it was a 50/50 chance to live if they operated on me
I was only 16, moms chose to opt out of surgery on me
to the street world I am now an outsider, inside me I'll forever
have a street life reminder

Flowers For The Dead

I got more friends dead than alive
sometimes I wish I was on the other side with
them
Ralphy first, Orlando, Bunca, then Edgar
sometimes when things get hard I point my head up and ask
God why?
thought things would get better it's not easy you see to be me
he took so many I grew up too early
but damn Lord, look at me, I'm clean
why not give them a chance to rejuvenate from the thirst of the
street dream
I ask, why didn't I die?
why are you keeping me around to see the tears falling from the
Rivas' the Lewis', Perez's, Morales'
and the Rosas' eyes?
when I see Denise and Cherly-lyn,
it reminds me of the first that went to heaven
I never got over that
since then, death been coming back to back
I log on FB and see the Rivas family by the dozens
nephews, nieces and cousins, sisters, mother and brother rest in
peace to daddy Bolo
since you went I know Orlando's not solo
the hardest female I know is my little sister, Jojo
bunca is no longer here for us to hold but through my eyes, he
see you grow
he sees you glow, he sees what you become, he sees his little
sister's baby son
Edie, it's not a coincidence we reconnected our connection to
your brother is something we both share, coexistence
Edgar could of killed someone and got the death penalty, the
electric chair
I would of switched seats at the last minute and let the current
run free through me
our bond was one level higher than family
if it wasn't for him taking one of the three shots that were
intended for me

Angel-Sade, Aaron and Jordan would never be calling me daddy

Knock, Knocked

knock, knock I'm getting paper
I got these fiends knocking at my door
I got duggie, girl or ready rock
what you want, I got it all
gat in hand, I open the door, dime slabs, give me four,
two dubs of powder and a bundle of duggie so I can speed ball
I like to be awake at times, then just like that my knuckle scraps the floor
this is how fiends order medication in illegal pharmaceutical stores
cop and go, keep it low, no whistles or noise in the halls
don't want my neighbors to make that 911 call
my door was right by the elevator
I heard it go up and down, down and up
I called it the patient escalator
I would hear a "ding", I knew it stopped
Footsteps, then the knock, either for the powder or the rock
there I am again opening the door, serving with one hand' other hand on my glock
I'm getting shoe box prezy's, my flow is deadly
with my hermanitos, we're grinding adding manito
or spinning that pyrex with my manito
less hammer more eina, lethal
I'm the local pusher like t, cold like ice
them chics I be having in those flux look like coco
I'm that Spanish kid in the bricks going loco
knock, knock I opened the door, I'm getting paper
I got these fiends knocking at my.... the cops kicked down my door
riot shields, mace, mask covering their face
"everybody down, everybody down"
couldn't hide nothing
guns and money, paraphernalia all around
my arms are behind my back, they're bound
dressers searched, then thrown to the ground
closets, cabinets searched

sofa cushions cut then flipped around
they seized pots, knives and spoons and other
utensils and tested it for a positive trace of coke
and dope residue
they found my safe after my finger prints were lifted
they called in a locksmith to pick it
just as they depicted, it's enough to put together a king
pin charge!
just yesterday....knock, knock
I'm getting paper
I got these fiends knocking on my door
I got duggie, girl or ready rock, what you want I
got it all
I"was" living large

Mask

you can't see my emotions because every few seconds I'm laughing and cheering
then the next few seconds, I'm sad so I'm tearing
my face remains the same throughout these senses
from my heart to my brain

I wear a mask

I can be the happiest man on earth jumping for joy
but I won't be smiling because of all the things I endured as a young boy
I can be the saddest man on earth mourning a moms first birth
I'll have the same look like I was jumping for joy because all the things I endured as a young boy

I wear a mask

over and over again I was happy and sad
sad then happy
it all started when I was twelve
I lost my daddy
I was happy before now I'm sad after
on my thirteenth birthday while blowing out candles, I was holding back tears
still blew out the candles for my happy peers
it hurt so much because pops wasn't here so the reason for me living another year wasn't clear
my visions of happiness disappeared

So I wear a mask

I lived in a project building, twelve stories
on each floor I knew about two children
so instead of knocking on each other's door
we had this made up call "skeeee youuuuuu"
in minutes from being just one kid now there's twenty-four
I'm so happy!

but, but, but, now I skeeee youuuuuuuuu
no one looks out the window from twenty four
how the hell in the world am I here solo?
I know, I know, I know, twenty three funerals
emotions up and down like a yo yo
I'm happy and sad sometimes I forget
I ask myself am I happy or sad?
I tell myself I don't know

I got used to wearing my mask!

Two Different Trips, Although Sounding Like Two Similar Stories

it was a lovely day, sitting in dads old station wagon with
the wood trim paneling
I'm sitting in the rear looking at all the traffic passing
the seat was facing outwards, facing towards the outskirts
of New York
I'm with my brothers and some friends screaming are
we there yet?
when will this trip end?
looking at the hills on the palisades, to us ghetto kids, those hills
are like the Everglades.....
we're on a trip upstate

my dad past away when I was twelve
now I'm fifteen, how quickly did I get to this point

it's a gloomy day
I'm in this big wagon with blue lettering on its side panel
dads not driving
I'm looking at the traffic passing
the seat was facing outwards, facing towards the outskirts
of New York
I'm with people who are not my brothers or friends screaming
are were there yet?
when will this trip end?
looking at the hills on the palisades, to us ghetto kids, those hills
are like the Everglades

we're on a trip to a juvy upstate

Veterans

some come back vets
some didn't come back at all
the last thing anyone heard about them was a letter or a final phone call
after years at war after this one life threatening battle, the next day they didn't make roll call
bombs bursting in the air, bang galore, bang galore
stepping over dead bodies to aim at Charlie
retrieving ammo cause they can no longer shoot at anybody
missing limbs, or no torso just legs in camo for tripping over trip wire and being riddled with shrapnel
some come out 730 for seeing blood fall out so many allies
dog chains they recovered about seven hundred and thirty
some look for a way out the unexplainable
they went in, as healthy as can be, they come out addicted to poppy seeds
some make it out with an honorable discharge
they walk around with combat boot and fatigues
when they hear a gun discharge they jump to the ground
calling in for a medevac but there's no walkie talkie or anyone around
after a few seconds they realize they're not at war anymore
march up to the corner store to drink away the war of yesterday
I know this well, my grandfather was an alcoholic veteran
my dad after his tour came out addicted to heroin
my uncle came out fine
God blessed him after many, many years being enlisted
I know many people just like them
some are able to tell me their story
some got military taps and hurried in Calverton's military cemetery

our veterans alive are our heroes so treat them as so!

Contact Information

If you would like to contact Al Carrasco, aka Infinite The Poet, you can contact him through email at:

alcarrasco2@yahoo.com

You can also call him for bookings at:

(646) 772-9433

Facebook:

http://facebook.com/alcarrasco2

You can look forward to seeing Al's second book sometime in 2013 released from Hip Hope Publishing. More info to follow.

www.ingramcontent.com/pod-product-compliance
Lightning Source LLC
LaVergne TN
LVHW091307080426
835510LV00007B/401